# "Guardian Angels Around My Bed"

## The Psychic life of Esoterical Psychologist

## Sally Jane Danter
### With
### Joy Cooke

## The Angel in the Wheelchair Ltd
## 31 Fulmar Road Rest Bay Porthcawl
## Mid-Glamorgan CF35 5RS

# "Guardian Angels Around My Bed"

On the second edition of my autobiography I believe that it is more important than the first, because on 13th May 1996, I will go in to hospital to have both legs amputated from six inches below the knee. So this time the publication of 'Guardian Angels Around My Bed' to my mother, friend Joy Cooke and I have decided that it is important for you all to know that my work and in particular this book will continue. I thank the 'Guardian Angels' once again for allowing me the strength and courage to carry on.

**Sally Jane Danter**

Production by MBC Consultancy
Typeset by BluePrint, Cambridge
Printed and bound in Great Britain by
JB Offset Printers, Marks Tey, Colchester

ISBN 1 898548 552

The Angel in the Wheelchair Ltd.

# CONTENTS

# ACKNOWLEDGMENTS

My heartfelt and everlasting thanks to my mother, Elizabeth, and all other members of my family and friends, in this world and the next, and to my co-writer, Joy Cooke, who have made my life, and this book, possible.

# FOREWORD
### From co-writer Joy Cooke

SALLY JANE DANTER is a most remarkable and courageous lady, who possesses extraordinary psychic gifts. It has given me such great pleasure and inspiration to have been so deeply involved with the preparation of this book. No one has made me realise more clearly than Sally Jane that even when faced with desperate and seemingly unsurmountable problems and situations there lies deep within ourselves a kind of secret ingredient – a superhuman, unshakeable determination which can be drawn upon, enabling us to achieve just about anything which we have set our heart and mind.

Countless numbers of sick, lonely and grieving people, from all walks of life, seek her help. Not only do they receive solace, guidance and healing, but they also find, in a lovely way, that life for them is never quite the same again.

Sadly, Sally Jane was born with a crippling spinal disorder and has undergone 24 major surgical operations during her 43 years. She is confined to a wheelchair, but in spite of all this, her whole life is devoted to using her God-given gifts to helping others.

From time to time articles about her work appear in the press. Tony Ortzen, editor of "Psychic News," has given his permission for two of these to be reproduced.

This one appeared in 1985. Headed, 'Wheelchair Sally still serves,' it reads:

BRAVE wheelchair-bound medium Sally Jane Danter is continuing to help others through her psychic work despite a health condition that has necessitated 22 operations.

Sally, 36, told PN she would have been unable to summon up the courage and endurance to make it through repeated surgery without the help and support of her guides, and in particular the presence of her grandfather who passed before she was born.

The Porthcawl, mid-Glamorgan, medium said that "pre-med" anaesthetics were often unnecessary because she felt no fear of pain when her guides reassure her all will be well.

"I've never met my grandfather in my life," said Sally, "yet I'm closer to him than many grandchildren whose grandfathers are still with them.

"I feel his presence every day. When I was in a plaster cast from my feet to my neck he was always with me. Before operations he always shows me how it will be."

When Sally was in hospital with a serious back complaint and an operation to straighten her spine was imminent, her grandfather appeared with others of Sally's guides to help ease her mind.

Sally sent PN a tape about her psychic work. A recent operation on her hands has made writing letters difficult and painful, she said.

Even as a child Sally was clairvoyant: she was frightened to talk about what she was "seeing" in case others dismissed it all as imagination.

On one occasion Sally saw the spirit form of an undertaker who said her grandmother would soon pass.

Five weeks later Sally knew her mind wasn't playing tricks when she was told her grandmother was dead.

Over the years many recipients have praised her mediumship.

A Mrs. Thomas, of Hoel-y-Parc, N. Cornelly, mid-Glamorgan, said: "We are not very often privileged to meet someone who impresses you as being a little angel in a frail human form. Sally lives her life in a wheelchair, giving comfort and solace to others when our loved ones return.

"My brother, who recently passed, communicated. I believe she has great gifts. She helped and comforted my sister-in-law and me."

Rita Pate, of Lon Eithen, Trehafren, Newtown, Powys, said her sceptical husband communicated in great detail through the medium.

"Though I have had correct messages from other mediums, this was the first time he mentioned one of my daughters by name," said Mrs Pate.

Sally feels the pain and suffering she has endured has given her fortitude and a better understanding of others' problem.

"I think that without the illness I would not have taken the time to take up the challenge of working for God in this cold world we live in, so something good has come out of it all.

"My illness has made me a strong-willed person. If I had not gone through it how could I have compassion for those who come to me for help?"

Of the future, Sally said: "My task is to work — and work hard — and be worthy of working for the spirit world.

"It's no good saying I shut the door because I am sick. I must give others who are sick the courage to continue their lives."

Three years later, this article was printed. It is reproduced in full:

MERELY by holding a photograph, a medium accurately described a suicide victim who passed in 1902.

Furthermore, Sally Jane Danter of Austin Avenue, Porthcawl, S Wales, reached back another 60 years to tell of the tragic demise of the victim's father — who shot himself with the flint-lock pistol which killed his young cousin.

The story was revealed to PN by sitter Leonard Taylor, who explained that he has been married to a gifted medium for many years, and was a member of the Society for Psychical Research and Spiritualist Association of Great Britain.

"I have had sittings with many mediums of varying ability and nationalities," he said.

"During that time I have never known greater accuracy and ability than that of Sally Jane. As a psychometrist, she is unsurpassed.

"I handed her a photograph of my paternal grandfather," Leonard explained.

"She accurately described his personal traits, his profession, the weakness that resulted in his suicide, the building and interior of the house concerned — and incredibly, the scene of horror behind the cellar door which greeted my father, then aged just 20."

Children in the house woke Leonard's parent when they could not get into the cellar. The door was blocked from inside.

Sally Jane described the suicide's father, a farmer in rural Essex, who also took his own life around 1842.

The medium gave the cause of the tragic act, "the strange old-fashioned flint-lock pistol with which he shot himself, the interior of the farmhouse — now demolished — and the fact that this pistol had been left to him by his young cousin who had previously killed himself with this same weapon."

What Leonard found most incredible was that the medium confirmed the great-grandfather had lain semi-conscious for eight hours that Sunday while a desperate search was made to locate a surgeon.

"Every detail has been fully ascertained by family research and details from coroners' reports examined by my brother and myself," testified Leonard, "some 20 years previously."

The sitter continued, "The incredible accuracy of this talented young medium is a startling reminder of the power of our very top mediums."

She has appeared at Stansted Hall, Essex, with Gordon Higginson and healer John Cain.

Sadly, Sally Jane is in continual acute pain from spinal deformity. She has undergone 24 major surgical operations during her 43 years, and is confined to a wheelchair.

"Only her amazing will-power and fixed intention to use her wonderful ability to aid and assist others enables her to continue her postal taped readings," Leonard said.

*Chapter One*

## VERY EARLY DAYS

MY mother, Elizabeth, clearly remembers the day I was born. Outside the house, in the little Welsh village of Maestag, it was bitterly cold and blustery, that November 1948. Inside, though, there was plenty of warmth, as loving family members, my grandmother and Auntie Doris, busied themselves in the next room, awaiting my birth.

It had been a premature and over-long labour. Everyone was thankful and delighted when the midwife came out of the bedroom with me in her arms smiling.

"Well, here she is," she said. "A tiny mite – just like a little doll."

Mama recalls how she sank back against her pillows utterly exhausted, eyes brimming over. Yet at that moment life seemed perfect, so blissfully unaware was she of what was to follow. However, during the night, suddenly waking from sleep, she experienced a terrible feeling of foreboding which she hastily brushed aside, telling herself it was through weakness after childbirth and meant nothing at all.

For the next next 16 days everything went busily along as it usually does when there is a new baby in the house. Because I was so tiny, Mama had to handle me with extra care, but nobody suspected there was anything wrong with me. One day, though, she noticed I seemed to be having breathing difficulties, and that my tiny body and limbs looked swollen.

Greatly alarmed, she called in the doctor, who immediately arranged for a specialist to examine me. He looked very grave as he said: "This child must be put into an incubator at once. You must have given her a great deal of care to have kept her alive until now. Thank goodness you had the good sense to act so promptly when you realised something was wrong."

I was taken straight away to a hospital in Cardiff and placed in an incubator. The doctors and nurses all told Mama later that her careful nursing and quick action had undoubtedly saved my life. I must say, here and now, that this same loving care has continued ever since. Without her help – and that of other members of my family – I would not have been able to function. For this I will always be eternally grateful.

Later I was transferred to London's Great Ormond Street Hospital, where the specialist gently broke the news to my parents that I had a serious curvature of the spine. This verdict was a devastating blow. When Mama asked him exactly how this would affect me, he replied: "Well, my dear, she'll never be able to walk without callipers and a special walking-aid, though as she grows older and stronger, we will be able to operate on her legs. For the present, though, I'm sorry to say there is nothing we can do."

Mama was so anxious to find something to help me that she began taking me to a private masseur, Jack Talvert, who massaged my limbs to help the circulation. He also instructed Mama how to continue the treatment at home. My grandma and Auntie Doris were always ready to help with this. In fact, as the months went by Auntie Doris became more like a second mother to me, always showering me with love.

From a very young age, even when I was still sleeping in the nursery with the "Teddy Bear" wallpaper, I could see spirit forms, but of course, I did not realise at that time that the people who came and stood by my bed, smiling down at me, were different from anyone else in the house. There was a nice old gentleman with white hair and blue eyes who came nearly every night. I would also see young children playing and laughing merrily, and chuckled with them until I fell asleep. You see, children are much nearer to the spirit world. Many parents know all about the "invisible playmates" that their youngsters find so real.

I suppose the fact that both my mother and grandmother were excellent psychics made it almost inevitable that I, too, would inherit the gifts, though until I was about four years old, nobody realised that I had.

These spirit people did not frighten me at all until one night my mother, awakened by my screams, rushed into my room and found me crying bitterly and very distressed. Cradling me in her arms she tried to calm me, saying I had had a "nasty dream" because she could make no sense at all of what I was trying to tell her between my sobs.

What I had seen was very frightening indeed – an extremely angry man beating two boys with a large piece of wood until they fell to the ground covered in blood. It was not until some years later that I found out what it all meant. Apparently, these two little children had been battered to death by their father who was hanged for his crime. The trauma of their horrific deaths kept pulling the spirits of both lonely, troubled little boys back to earth. In later years their dead father came to me, full of remorse, begging me to tell him how he could find forgiveness. All three of those poor souls needed to be rescued. I will explain all about this in a later chapter.

For many months the old gentleman came nightly. One day he said: ".I am your grandfather, Edward, my angel. Never be afraid of anything. I will always watch over you."

This was my father's father who had passed into spirit life four years before I was born so I never actually saw him on earth, but later recognised him when shown family photographs. But "Grampy Danter," our family name for him, is just one of the many "guardian angels" I always see around me.

## Chapter Two

## MY PSYCHIC DEVELOPMENT BEGINS

WHEN I was about four years old, my father became terribly short-tempered and restless. The strain and weight of his responsibilities became more than he could bear, so he simply walked away from them . . . and us! This is all I intend to say on the subject.

From then onwards, Mama was more grateful than ever for the help given her by grandma and Auntie Doris. It enabled her to carry on more easily with her business life, running a hairdressing salon. Mama is a wonderful hairdresser and has always kept my hair in perfect condition.

One morning not long after the dreadful upset of my father's departure, I was sitting beside the window playing with my toys when out of the corner of my eye I saw a man dressed in dark, sombre clothing walking past. "Come quickly, Nanna, and see this funny man," I called out.

My grandma, who was looking after me that day, came running into the room and stood beside me. She at once recognised the "funny man" to be the spirit form of the undertaker who used to live across the road and who had passed into spirit life some years earlier. She was absolutely amazed when I said, "Don't be afraid, Nanna, it's only a spirit of nature, you know." And, of course, she realised I was psychic.

There was great excitement when Mama returned home and was told all about it.

From that day onwards, both Mama and grandma – they were also psychics – made it their loving duty gently to steer me through the various stages of my psychic development. Enthralled, I would sit listening as they explained the existence of the spirit world, that is, an unseen world all around us, and of guardian angels (to use the biblical term) or guides, who are able to come to us, and are always ready to offer help, comfort and guidance, if only we allow them to do so.

There were so many questions I wanted them to answer. All this seemed to prompt in me a kind of vague spiritual awakening as if reminding me of something which was not really new to me, rather like somebody reading me a story I had heard before.

When a person has inherited psychic gifts and is trained by someone who also possesses such capabilities the development takes place naturally of all the gifts – clairvoyance, clairaudience, psychometry, aura readings and healing. There has never been a need for me to join a Spiritualist church development circle, which is the usual way.

Most people are born with latent psychic capabilities, but as with great opera singers, musicians and painters, special training is necessary to bring out their full potential, so that their God-given gifts can be used for the benefit of others

The months went by. It was during one of the periods of instructions and meditation with Mama and grandma that a lovely young woman appeared before us in the room, sitting in an old-type basket wheelchair. She had light brown hair flowing over her shoulders and down her back, and lovely brown eyes. Her long dress was of a delicate lilac coloured material. On her head she wore a large picture hat. Smiling at me she said: "Hello, Sally Jane. I am Victoria Beaumont. I have come to tell you that when I was on earth my spine was like yours, so I understand exactly how you feel. I will come to see you again soon." Then she slowly faded from sight.

All the time she was there, I experienced a kind of choking sensation in my throat which remained for some minutes. In later months I found out why this was. Victoria came to us on many occasions and later became one of my most helpful guides. Many other people have seen her standing next to me, such as Mama's mediumistic friends, and even some doctors and nurses when I was in hospital.

Years later a lovely thing happened which gave me proof that other people could see Victoria exactly as I see her. One evening when I was giving a demonstration on a church rostrum there happened to be a psychic artist present. Unbeknown to me, she was sketching away all the time I was in deep conversation with someone. Afterwards she came over and handed me a coloured portrait saying: "Do you know who this lady is? She has been standing beside you ever since you came in."

I was absolutely amazed when I looked at it, for there, smiling up at me, was Victoria, exactly as I had always been used to seeing her!

Psychic artists do a very valuable job, for their work gives visual proof that spirit people do exist, and are perfectly capable of communicating with us. When the psychic artist draws a sketch of a spirit being she is seeing, and it is easily recognisable to someone who is grieving over a loved one, what wonderful joy this brings them to know they are *not* gone and lost for ever.

In the beginning Victoria's appearances to us were short, but gradually she told us all about her own life and death. This is what she said:

"When I was a young child my back was weak. It would pain me if I ran around too much when at play with my friends, so I had to rest.

"Later, as I grew older and stronger, it seemed to become much better. When John and I met and fell in love, we married and for a time had a very happy life living in London. When our little daughter was born John and I were overjoyed, but soon afterwards he had to leave us to go and fight in the Boer War.

"I was so miserable without him, but my mother was there to help me look after little Sally (Yes, Sally Jane, her name was Sally like yours). One afternoon news was brought to us that poor John had been killed in action. I could not believe we would never see each other again. I just could not get over it. My back seemed to be affected by my desperate loneliness and misery. It became so painful I had to have an operation. This left me so weak I was unable to walk so mother would push me around in a wheelchair. So you can see, Sally Jane, how it is that I understand exactly how you feel.

"I became worse, had to stay in my bed all the time and could hardly eat because of a choking sensation I would have when I tried to swallow. My mother tried to coax me to take a little food by breaking up small pieces of bread and placing them carefully in my mouth, but I had a choking spasm and the food stuck in my throat. The last thing I can remember of my passing was the heartbroken despair on my poor mother's face. But when I came to this beautiful place John was waiting and greeted me fondly, and all the family is with me now. I am happy once again."

Victoria's story explained to me the reason for those choking sensations I experienced on each occasion she had appeared to us. My psychic sensitivity picked up her last feelings on earth.

It was some time later that Victoria told me the other reason why she had come to me.

Months later during one of our peaceful meditation sessions Victoria came to us again, saying, "Today, Sally Jane, I will tell you something that will teach you more about yourself."

Suddenly, by her side there appeared what I can only describe as a kind of "reflection" of a pretty little girl. She was wearing a long white dress tied with a large pink ribbon bow long pantaloons and small white button-up boots. Her dark hair was curled into ringlets whilst her eyes were brown. She was sweetly smiling.

"This was how my daughter, Sally, used to look, and as you see her, Sally Jane, you are really looking at yourself for you were she in your life before."

We were all delighted at this revelation and my curiosity being so aroused that I wanted to know more and more. It is quite a strange sensation coming face to face with one's self in this way!

Victoria went on: "When I was so ill, and had to be pushed around in my wheelchair, little Sally seemed fascinated with it and would want to sit on my lap to ride with me. She kept asking me to get a small one just for her.

"Many years after her passing into this beautiful spirit world the time came for her to decide what kind of life she would choose when reborn on earth. She chose, or you chose, your present one."

By this time I had been told all about the laws of reincarnation, and, so did, in fact, learn a great deal from Victoria about myself and the reason for my kind of life.

*Chapter Three*

## ABOUT KARMA AND REINCARNATION

VERY often people ask me to tell them about these subjects. I try to do so as simply as possible, but there are many wonderful books, easily available, which explain them in depth.

It seems generally assumed that karma and reincarnation refer only to Oriental teachings and, therefore, do not relate to us in our everyday life. In actual fact, they are really of the greatest importance to everyone. Karma means action, but I think it would be more easily understood if we looked upon it as results of our actions.

When we die, our soul leaves the body and passes to a different dimension on a much higher frequency where, in most cases, it is reunited with all the people we loved on earth who have gone before. I say "in most cases" because there are exceptions about which I will explain later. After a time of adjustment and healing – if this is necessary – the soul is given the opportunity after perhaps many, many years of choosing another life on earth.

It is reborn in the body of a baby to live another earthly life – with all its traumas, happiness, pain and sorrows so that it will learn many lessons and gain by the experiences and knowledge that it absorbs during that time.

This is reincarnation. The reason for it all is from the moment we are born, and reborn, what is known as the Universal Law of Cause and Effect starts to operate.

Each and every one of our emotions and thoughts – whether they be good or bad – and our mistakes are imprinted upon our soul. Good deeds and helpful actions towards others will make a good karma, but evil thoughts and deeds will build a bad karma. These bad things will bring about a karmic debt which must be "repaid" or "cleansed" before our progress can be continued towards more spiritual levels.

Just as in nature, when all things planted in the earth struggle to the surface to find the sun, so is our soul forever reaching out towards the light of spirit. The only way, therefore, to improve our karma is to return to earth time after time in an effort to erase those "blots on our copybook" which are impeding our spiritual progress.

We have all been given complete free will. Before each incarnation we are shown by spirit what possible spiritual advancement a certain life could offer us, but it is completely our own choice as to what kind of life we will lead. Whether we choose to take the "high road" or the "low road" is entirely our own responsibility.

Sometimes, if we choose a very difficult, painful life, but one which could bring us more knowledge, and at the same time, be a means of benefit to others, our karmic debt would be much more quickly repaid, allowing us to go forward spiritually.

My karma in this life is to be confined to a wheelchair with a crippling spinal disorder, so that I may learn exactly what it means to have constant restriction and pain. How else could I fully understand the pain and suffering of those who come to me for help and be able to offer them love and compassion?

In spite of all my personal restrictions, thankfully, through my God-given psychic gifts, I am able to help many people. These gifts completely compensate.

I would say emphatically that to be born with a crippling disability is not the end of the world – it is tragic, yes, but through all adversity it is possible to overcome many things if one has parents strong enough to take up the challenge – and remember, most disabled people are compensated by having various talents, which bring joy to others. Here, I am thinking of such wonderful people as foot and mouth artists, and friends of mine who are marvellous knitters and create beautiful garments, also others who are so gifted musically that listening to them is pure delight.

Over the years, in my work as a spiritual healer, I have had the joy of seeing the gratitude felt by people who have been freed from their pain. Some of them have looked at me in my wheelchair and said sadly, "Sally Jane, you are able to heal so many, why can't you heal yourself?"

I ask them to sit down in the peace of my sanctuary, and try to explain that it is just not possible for me to do this. One healer must be healed by another healer. In my case, in spite of the fact that Mama has asked many healers to treat me, as soon as they see me they realise that a cure is not possible, because mine is a karmic condition, which must be endured throughout my life for my soul's sake.

## Chapter Four

## SCHOOLDAYS

THE time came when I needed to be educated so it was arranged for me to have an IQ test.

I remember sitting before Professor Watkins, the educational psychologist, answering his many questions. The little dress I was wearing had a pattern of half moons and stars. Professor Watkins pointed at them and asked, "Sally Jane, can you tell me where you think stars come from?"

Without hesitation, I replied, "They come from the universe." He then asked, "What do you do with a ball?" I answered, "I throw it."

Then the professor asked, "What do you do with an orange?" My prompt reply was, "I eat it."

On our way home I complained to Mama: "Why did Professor Watkins ask me such silly questions? I'm not a baby."

Obviously, though, my answers were the right ones, because the professor had said to Mama: "Well, Mrs Danter, you need have no worries about this child's intelligence. She's as bright as a button and will need a good education."

Because of my disability it was necessary for me to go to a special bording school for children like myself where I would receive education and physiotherapy on my legs.

Unfortunately, at the school I just could not settle down and found it a very difficult and unhappy 11 months, but so as not to worry Mama I never told her how I felt.

One afternoon as I was preparing to go down for physiotherapy and feeling very downhearted, Grampy Danter appeared in my room. Smiling kindly at me he said, "My little angel (he always called me that), don't you think it is time you told your mother how unhappy you are here, for she really would want to know?"

So I did tell Mama . . . who promptly took me away from there. My next school was a mixed one in Penarth. Here I boarded weekdays and was taken home at weekends.

The headmaster was a good, kind man who always encouraged and impressed it upon us all that in spite of our disabilities we were people of high intellect and would be able to go forward in life if we made up our minds to take up the challenge.

My Grandparents Danter had not lived with, or even near us, because they were travelling show people in charge of catering. They were well respected all over Wales, especially in Cardiff, travelling with the fun fair. After Grampy Danter died, grandma still continued with the work she loved, but would come to visit us whenever she possibly could. I used to feel, though, that she found it very difficult to accept my disability, almost convincing herself that I would grow out of it.

I remember that during one of those visits, as I was about to start school, she told me: "You must do well in school and get to the top, Sally Jane. You must just not sit back and waste yourself. Always remember that."

No matter how much pain I was feeling, I always tried to go forward.

Neither Mama nor I ever mentioned my psychic capabilities to anyone there, because we felt they were unlikely to understand these matters, so when I had psychic experiences, I simply kept them to myself.

My family and I soon settled down to the routine of my being away all week and home at weekends, when Mama and my grandmother would continue with my psychic development. I was rapidly becoming competent in reading the aura.

Victoria became a regular visitor as was, of course, Grampy Danter, who would bring other spirit beings to greet us.

On one memorable occasion he brought a very dignified elderly gentleman, with long white hair and brown eyes. His skin was tanned as if he had come from a very sunny climate.

"This is Saint Saba," said Grampy. "He will be at your side whenever he knows you have need of him."

Now neither Mama nor grandmother or I had ever heard of this particular saint, but we greeted him and thanked him warmly, feeling quite honoured by his presence. I had instantly recognised him, though, for he had appeared to me many times, standing beside my bed, not speaking, but smiling down at me with kindly eyes.

Saint Saba spoke very quietly and gently to me: "My child, I have been watching over you since the day you came into this dark world and will always be near you. When you are ready I will instruct you in many spiritual things, so that you may go forward to do the work for which you were born – helping humanity."

He then told us briefly of his own life's work and of the monastery called Mar Saba, built in a wild valley between Jerusalem and the Dead Sea, and which is still inhabited today.

My development continued, even during the days I was at school. At night, when the other children lay sleeping, Saint Saba would come to instruct me in many things which would be needed to further my development. He explained the real need for fasting before communication with spirit beings takes place, for in so doing, this leaves an "empty channel" for them. He also gave me instruction in philosophy. With him I had my first experience of astral travel, known as an O.O.B.E. (out-of-body experience). This occurs in the sleep state, when the spirit temporarily leaves the body and is able to visit many places, both in this world and the next.

I can remember clearly standing with Saint Saba outside the old stone walls of a monastery. Through the gate I could see a cool courtyard, but Saint Saba explained that it was not permitted for me, a female, to enter.

Saint Saba taught me that within us all there is a golden key to happiness. All this wonderful spiritual knowledge that he gave me I am now able to impart to my own students.

By now I was becoming so familiar with the colours of the aura of each child in school that I knew instinctively which ones would go forward and do well, and those who would at a young age pass into the next world.

There was no one else in the school who was psychic so I was unable to discuss with anyone the inner knowledge I possessed. I cannot imagine how my life would be without Saint Saba, this kind, gentle spirit mentor, who in his own lifetime experienced all the struggles of mankind.

I am truly proud and thankful that he came to me and my family, and for the inner strength his presence gives me when I am treating difficult cases.

One of my most treasured possessions is a sketch of Saint Saba drawn when I was giving a church demonstration. The psychic artist handed this to me, saying: "I can see this man standing beside you. He tells me that his name is Saba."

I was delighted to have a very life-like picture of my spiritual teacher. Once again the skill of the psychic artist proved to me that others see him exactly as I do.

Some years ago, when I switched on the television, I saw the opening captions of a documentary. Mama had just gone into the kitchen to make a cup of tea. I called out excitedly: "Come quickly, Mama. Look, it's all about Saint Saba and his monastery."

She hurried back into the room and we both sat in utter amazement and joy as the presenter was telling of the Saint's life and work. There, before our eyes, was Mar Saba.

It was wonderful actually to see the courtyard I had so often seen on my astral travels and to go right inside, for visitors are now welcomed. It is always so rewarding for me when I am given confirmation of things which have been revealed to me by Spirit. Knowing that so many dedicated guides and guardian angels are ever present gives me such comfort and confidence. This is not in any way "guide worship" because I know that they, as well as I, work only for God and humanity.

Being so aware of their presence in times of trouble, and sometimes fear, is vital to me. There have been countless instances of this in my lifetime. I remember one occasion when there was an outbreak of dysentery at school which affected me badly, most probably because I had previously been sitting with a little boy who was in the sickbay. This I would do whenever possible because he seemed to be so unhappy and lonely and I tried to cheer him up.

So ill did I become that it was decided to send me to the isolation hospital. My mother had to be sent for. There I was lying terribly ill in bed when Sister brought her in. I took one look at Mama's worried face and thought in panic, "They've brought her here because they think I'm going to die."

But I held back my tears until they had gone out of the room. Then the floodgates opened. In great distress and fear I beseeched: "Oh, God, please don't let me die. My life has only just begun. I don't want to go."

Suddenly there was Grampy Danter beside me, smiling. "Hush, Pet, don't upset yourself," he said. "I promise soon you will be well again."

I was so relieved for I knew well that if Grampy said it would be so, then it would be. Shortly afterwards a young doctor came towards me smiling and saying, "Cheer up, Sally Jane, you're going to be fine."

As he spoke I was fascinated to see all around his head the beautiful colours of his aura. This showed him to be a truly caring and dedicated man. I slept well that night, and soon recovered.

In spite of everything, my schooldays were happy ones. We children would all help each other, and I made many friends. Each child there, though, had a disability. Some were very delicate so it was inevitable that, at times, we would "lose" one to the spirit world.

At these times it was fortunate for me that Grampy Danter would make his presence strongly felt, helping me to accept the loss. He comforted me by saying: "Don't fret, my angel. Be happy that your little friend is now out of pain and will be with people she loves."

I remember one little girl named Ann, a delightful child who suffered from muscular dystrophy, and was very frail indeed. Her father, a veterinary surgeon, would bring her to school each day. She looked like a pretty little doll in her red hat, coat and leggings. Little Ann loved to be with us but because of her weak condition could only stay for a few hours daily. Her mother would not allow her to board.

Every week after school we would have a Brownie meeting and Ann would be allowed to stay for it. On this particular day it had been snowing hard since early afternoon and had settled quite thickly on the ground. I was sitting talking to Ann when to my surprise she began to cry, sobbing, "I want my Daddy."

The house mother, looking anxiously out of the window at the snow-covered road, said, "Wouldn't you like to stay here with us tonight, dear?" But the little girl was quite definite and said emphatically: "No! I want my Daddy." There was no consoling her. In due course, however, up drove her loving father in his little red Mini and carried her out to the car. We all waved as it disappeared down the drive, leaving deep tracks behind. We never saw Ann again, but heard soon afterwards that she had died of pneumonia.

This is not the end of the story, for some months later during one of our family development sessions Ann suddenly appeared in our midst. Smiling, she said: "Sally Jane, you used to be so kind to me at school. People here are showing me how I will be able to come and help you when you are ready."

Nowadays, she always comes when I am treating patients with serious disabilities, and people with asthma.

## Chapter Five

## HOSPITAL DAYS

AT school, it was the doctor's decision as to which child should receive physiotherapy. At first I was given some, but later, when the treatment seemed not to be helping me, this was discontinued.

One weekend, when Mama was helping me to bath, she noticed a lump on my spine. Now this was something completely new, and alarming. Mama could hardly wait to report it to the school doctor when she took me back there on Monday.

In bed that night Grampy Danter and Saint Saba came to tell me not to worry even though I would need to go to hospital as they would be there with me and all would be well.

Upon examining me, the doctor said, "I think the time has come for Sally Jane to undergo an operation on her knees and the backs of her legs."

I entered the hospital in Cardiff. On the day of my operation, as I was being pushed along towards the theatre, I could see Grampy Danter and Saint Saba walking along beside the nurses – and felt no fear.

This was the first of 10 operations carried out by Dylan Evans in the following months. Up to the present time I have had 24 major operations, 10 by Mr Evans, one by Richard Cotterel and the rest by David Jenkins. I am deeply grateful to all those skilful and dedicated surgeons, doctors and nurses to whom I owe so much.

After the first operation my legs were put in plaster for some time. When this was taken off the physiotherapist lowered me into a hydrotherapy pool. This was a wonderful experience, for my limbs felt so relaxed and weightless.

Then began the difficult and painful days of learning to walk. Physiotherapists would slowly walk up and down with me. To everyone's delight gradually, for the first time in my life, at the age of 16, with the help of a walking aid I was able to move about unaided.

This new independence of mine was so wonderful, and at home I could move slowly around the bungalow. It was, indeed, a new life for me.

It was when I was in hospital, recovering from one of my operations, that I met Karen. In those days, I could manage to wash myself and was busy doing this behind my bed curtains when I heard a dreadful commotion – a young girl was screaming pitifully. It was Karen. She had been in a terrible car accident, leaving her with spinal injuries and a broken neck. It was necessary for her to have weights put on the top of her head in order to keep it perfectly still and firmly in place. She was begging the doctor and nurses not to do it because the pain was so great.

Later that day, I sat with her and tried to stop her from crying. As time went by, we became such good friends that Sister even pushed our beds together. The only time we separated was when Karen had to be turned over.

I remember one day in particular when Karen was in great discomfort and pain. She said to me, "Do you think I will ever get better, Sally Jane?"

"Of course you will," I replied quickly. "Don't be silly." But it was a white lie, because I saw the dark grey of her aura becoming more dense, and I knew perfectly well what that meant.

Every visiting time my relations would come. We were delighted to see that Karen had so many friends, all bringing gifts, sometimes as many as 14 in one night! One evening her boy friend brought her a lovely royal blue dressing gown and pale blue nightdress. She was delighted, saying, "When I am well again, I will be able to wear them instead of this awful theatre gown."

The nurse hung them up in her wardrobe. But Karen never had the opportunity of seeing herself dressed in those pretty clothes.

We spent seven months together in that hospital. On the day I was released Karen asked Mama and my aunt to lift her up a little for me to kiss her goodbye. I felt so terribly sad because I knew I would never see her alive again.

Shortly after this, Mama took me on a visit to America. Whilst there, we received a letter from Karen's mother telling us that her poor daughter had died. She dressed her in the royal blue dressing gown and pale blue nightdress that Karen had longed to wear.

Many mediums in various Spiritualist churches have since seen the spirit of Karen near me. A psychic artist drew a sketch of her.

Karen was 15 years old when she died. What a lovely friend she was, one who most certainly enriched my life. She now works with me as a guide.

Several times I have mentioned seeing a person's aura. For the benefit of those who do not know what this means I will give a brief explanation.

Around every single living thing there is a magnetic field which radiates in various colours and looks rather like a rainbow. All these colours have a different meaning and can change with a person's mood. From them, the highly sensitive medium is able to interpret correctly and assess state of health, feelings, hopes and fears.

For instance, in a person who is spiritually undeveloped their colours will extend to a width of about five to six inches in murky reds and browns and will appear to be unstable. In a highly spiritual person, however, their aura will have beautiful, bright colours, predominantly royal blue, and are of a permanent and constant vibration, extending several feet.

Around doctors and healers I always see a lot of pale greens and many other lovely hues.

Orange will denote that a person has a strong inner driving force to lead others. Our previous Prime Minister's aura has much orange and deep purple showing that she is a very strong lady indeed.

Pink denotes a really loving personality, while white shows pure thoughts. Pale blue denotes that a person has periods of "blues." Black will appear in the aura of a split personality or schizophrenic.

To be able to read a person's aura is a very valuable asset to a medium, for it gives an instant assessment of so many things.

## Chapter Six

### WE VISIT AMERICA

WHEN I was 15 Mama arranged for us to go to the United States. This was intended to serve two purposes – a lovely holiday with many new experiences for me and an opportunity for Mama to consult American surgeons, hopefully to find out if there was anything new they could do to help my condition. So far the operations and physiotherapy I had undergone made it possible for me to walk slowly indoors with the help of an aid, but I still needed a wheelchair to go any distance.

Auntie Doris and my cousin Paul came with us on the train from Cardiff to Southampton. As the ship would not be setting sail until midnight we had time to look around the town and have a meal before going on board the S.S. France, a beautiful liner, one of the largest in the world.

I could hardly contain my excitement as we all sat in the lounge-bar drinking champagne until it was time for Auntie Doris and cousin Paul to leave us and go ashore. They wrote to us later and told us how they stood watching with a large lump in their throats until the ship became a mere speck on the horizon.

The four-night, five-day sea journey to New York proved to be exhilarating. I enjoyed every moment of it except for an occasional feeling of apprehension when I stopped to think that, huge as she was, the S.S. France was still only a spot on the deep, deep ocean!

As we approached New York in the early hours of the morning we were awakened by the stewards to see the Statue of Liberty. It was an amazing sight, all lit up.

After disembarking we were driven to the John F. Kennedy Airport. On the way, we passed some really poverty-stricken and seedy areas, especially Harlem. Our taxi driver smiled ruefully and said, "Harlem is not a safe place to walk alone, honey." I thought to myself, "Well even if I could I certainly wouldn't want to."

It was rather frightening to see all the police with guns in their belts, but this was the darker side of life which exists in most large cities.

We had a long wait at the airport, because our flight was not leaving until the evening. Mama went to buy us a cup of coffee. As I sat there in my wheelchair looking all around suddenly there was a scuffle. Two men, who we were told later were private detectives, rushed towards a man, pushed him to the ground and handcuffed his wrists. Mama came back, but missed the excitement. People there told us that it was an unusual thing to happen in front of everyone. To us, it was just like watching a TV movie.

We settled down comfortably, Mama looking at an American magazine and I watching drowsily as people passed to and fro. Suddenly, I felt the spirit presence of Frankie, a US Marine, who was killed in the war when his ship was torpedoed. Saint Saba brought him to me when I was about five years old because Frankie had asked if he could be my "Protector." Sometimes he used to bring his little daughter, Lolly, to see me. Frankie told me how desperately sad he had felt when she died just before he had joined his ship. Now he stood grinning broadly at me and said, "It's great that we are together here on my own ground."

I asked him if he would prefer to stay here in America to protect someone else, but he shook his head, saying, "No, no, my work is to protect you, Sally Jane, and I'm happy doing just that!"

I thanked Frankie and told him how very pleased I was to have his help.

After the night flight to Dayton, Ohio, we travelled by road to Indiana, passing some lovely houses and beautiful gardens – such a contrast to those we had seen in Harlem. Our journey ended at my aunt's house, where we would be staying.

Because I was eager to meet young Americans of my own age, I applied to enter the Joseph Moore School, but before they would accept me it was necessary to take a test set by an educational psychologist. Mama and I were so pleased to hear that I had passed with flying colours.

The school was not a special one, but it did have a separate classroom solely for disabled children. During free periods we were all encouraged to mix with the pupils in the main part of the building. They were all very friendly, and there was a wonderful rapport between my school teacher, Miss McKinney and myself, that made learning a real joy. If ever there is an opportunity, I should like to go back to the school to see her again.

In America school hours start very early in the day. Lessons are finished by 2.30 pm which gives everyone more time for leisure pursuits.

Every afternoon Mama and I travelled by taxi to the hospital where I received physiotherapy. Afterwards we would go sightseeing to many interesting places.

Being from Wales, everyone went out of their way to make our stay a happy one by arranging several nice surprises for me. For instance, one morning the Mayor of Indiana came and handed me a key brooch, which was rather like being given the Freedom of the City!

Another time, I had the great pleasure of meeting a Red Indian chief who came into the school in all his colourful splendour, wearing a beautiful feathered head-dress and a fringed leather tunic. What a lovely aura that man had, showing him to be a strong but loving personality.

He showed me a tiny pair of moccasins which had been worn by a young girl many years ago. As I held them in my hands, such an intense feeling of sadness and despair surged through me that I handed them back to him quickly, unable to say a word. The chief began telling us a little about the life of his ancestors in "the far off times" and how many of them were massacred by the soldiers. I then realised the reason for my feelings of depression.

He spoke so sadly of his anger at the way American westerns depicted the people of the Great Indian Nation in such a bad light. Sighing heavily he said, "Always remember, it was the white man who took our lands and our dignity, which made our young men rebel and were forced to fight a losing battle for their freedom." It moved me deeply.

We stayed in America for seven-and-a-half months. During that time President Kennedy and Martin Luther King were assassinated. It was impossible not to be affected by the shocked outrage felt by all the people. We were saddened that such a good man as Martin Luther King, like so many others, should be killed for their beliefs.

Many years afterwards, when sitting quietly meditating in my sanctuary, Martin Luther King appeared before me and said, "You will speak of me to a congregation of people." Then he disappeared. I wondered how this could come about, but within a few weeks I was invited to be the guest speaker at a lovely little Tabernacle in the Rhonda Valley.

Up on the rostrum, in my wheelchair beside the minister, he said to me: "Sally Jane, I would like you to take the service. I know you are quite capable of doing it."

Thanking him, I began to compose myself in readiness and immediately became aware of the presence of Martin Luther King. Clairvoyantly his words poured into my mind. I began, "Tonight, my friends, I want to talk about Martin Luther King and man's inhumanity to man," and continued fluently, with great confidence.

Afterwards, people came to congratulate me on a very inspiring talk and commented that they had witnessed a remarkable change come over me – my features, my mannerism, even to the darkness of my skin – almost as if I had been taken over by someone else! Since that day, Martin Luther King has come to me many times on such occasions.

One afternoon, when Mama and I were out sight-seeing in Indiana, we went into a little church. Mama pushed my wheelchair to the front. She sat down on the bench and we quietly prayed. When the first hymn was being sung both of us were amazed to hear the strength and enthusiasm of the voices, joyously singing God's praises. Smiling, Mama and I looked over our shoulders and saw that every member of that congregation was Black. All the beautiful colours of the aura were around each one. Everywhere there was a wonderful atmosphere of love.

After the sermon, some of the congregation came up to us, smiling broadly and shaking us by the hand. One of them spoke, saying: "Two white ladies in our Black church. You must be loving people." We were very surprised at his words. I remarked: "But this is a church, isn't it? Anyone can come in to pray?"

The man looked so sad as he replied: "No, honey. The White church is across the road." He told us about the situation that existed in the country.

Mama and I thought that it was a dreadfully sad state of affairs, that these Black people would suffer such humiliation and rejection from their fellow men.

As the worshippers were leaving, we sat a little while longer. Quite suddenly we both had a wonderful experience. There was a change in the vibrations around us, which became so highly charged as to make our limbs quiver as if in high excitement. Tears of emotion filled our eyes. A man's spirit voice spoke, saying: "Remember all that you have witnessed today. In spite of the degradations these people suffer, their belief in God allows them to rise above it all and to carry on with their lives. All this, you will also come to know. But Spirit is ever close and will help you to go forward. It will never let you down." Some time later I had good reason to remember those words . . .

The American surgeon at the hospital in Indiana told us he would be able to help me by carrying out a bone graft on my spine. We would need to get a visa to stay in the United States for four years, but unfortunately were unable to get permission to stay for that length of time. Had it been possible, there would have been no reason for me to have undergone several serious and painful operations later on in life.

It was getting towards the end of our holiday so we decided to visit Chicago, "The Windy City." On our way back to Indiana a tornado hit us, which was a very frightening experience. Great flashes of lightning lit up the sky, the heavens opened and huge hailstones the size of golf balls bombarded us. One of our friends gathered some of these and when she got home put them into her freezer to show people. Someone asked us, "Don't you ever get storms like this in England?" We were pleased to reply, "Thankfully, no!" We had never experienced anything like it in our lives.

All too soon the time came for us to embark on the S.S. France again to go home. What a wonderful reception we were given by the captain and crew, who had remembered us! When we eventually arrived home, there were lots of hugs and kisses from relatives and friends. For some weeks afterwards my thoughts remained crowded by all we had seen and done.

*Chapter Seven*

## NEW BEGINNINGS

EVER since my development began, from time to time I had psychic experiences. After our holiday, these became even more frequent.

I remember on one occasion when Mama and I went to stay with Auntie Doris and my two cousins, Peter and Paul. She and I slept in a double bed in a large room. During the night we were awakened by the presence of a monk. He had red cheeks, smiling eyes, and a gentle manner.

"I am Father Thomas," he said. "I will be coming to help you later on." Then he disappeared.

Next morning we were all getting ready to go out when quite suddenly my wheelchair – with me in it – rose into the air and was gently rocked. Auntie Doris, in alarm, turned on Paul, who was standing close beside me, and shouted: "What on earth do you think you're doing? You'll hurt Sally Jane."

Poor Paul was so taken aback by what he had just witnessed that he stammered: "But I didn't do anything, Mum. The chair just lifted up itself."

Mama and I could see Father Thomas with his hands grasping the handles. "I don't like to see you in this thing," he said. "I want you to be fit and well."

He didn't like my chair, but most certainly meant me no harm. In fact, he has since come back to me many times and has proved to be a loving, caring guide.

Another time, some friends took me to a lovely park. As they were pushing me along the pathways, edged with flower borders, I looked across the smooth green stretches of grass and it was difficult to realise that at one time, beneath it all, there had once been a coalmine. I began to sense strongly the spirit beings of two poor souls who had perished in a pit accident. The spirit form of a heavily built man walked over and told me his name was John. The other one, a younger thin lad joined us, walking alongside.

"My mate, Dave here, was trapped with me down the mine, after a fall," he explained. "We tried to hack our way out along the tunnel, and could even see a bit of daylight up ahead. We thought we were saved, but down came another load of rocks, burying us deep. So that was that – and we both came over here. It's good thing I did, because my legs were badly crushed. If I had lived, being without legs is something I just couldn't have faced."

The expression on Dave's face, though, was one of sadness and bewilderment. They then gradually faded from sight. Neither of my friends were aware of the two spirit forms, thinking that I was sitting silently, quietly enjoying the pleasant surroundings.

At first when things like this happened to me, I felt strange, as if I were living in two worlds at the same time, but gradually I came to accept it naturally.

At the end of my schooldays, my teacher's mother, also a psychic, invited me to tea. She realised very quickly how strong were my psychic capabilities, and told me: "Sally Jane, I can see that you have been very well blessed with spiritual gifts. One day you will use them to help thousands of people."

I replied eagerly, "Yes, I know, but *when* will it all happen?"

The gentle lady smiled quietly at my obvious impatience, promising, "It will happen, my dear, when you are truly ready."

So I had to try to content myself with that. Not long after this, however, Saint Saba came to me, saying: "Have patience, little one. You will meet a gentleman who will help you to go forward."

After hearing these words, every time any man came into casual contact with my family I would study him carefully, searching for some sign that it were he!

Soon my schooldays came to an end. In spite of my disability it had been a really interesting and active time for me, during which I studied drama, art, music and poetry. Reading poetry out loud proved to be excellent training for a future time when I was addressing congregations from the rostrum. Also, my friends used to take me with them to pop concerts and theatres, so I was able to do most things that teenagers enjoy.

All these activities taught me self-confidence. We were always encouraged to travel alone whenever possible, using taxis, trains, etc., so we would become more independent should we be left without parents at some future time.

Many of my schoolfriends are now in the spirit world, but often appear to me. I am actually seeing one of them now, as I write. Her name is Margaret. She was much older than me and left school a good deal earlier, but after a time, returned to work as a young housemother. Margaret met, and fell in love with a teacher. They married and had a lovely baby, but tragically she had to go into hospital for a heart operation and passed away. Every time Margaret appears to me, she wears the orange dress she made in our sewing class. I helped her to choose the colour because she couldn't decide.

After we came back from our holiday in America, Mama did not return to her business life straightaway and would invite several of her friends, some of them psychics, home for tea. Often they would say to me, "You know, Sally Jane, soon you will have to do something about your gifts, because you could help so many people."

I knew this to be true, but eager as I was to begin, inwardly knew that things would have to wait a little longer until the time was right.

Meanwhile, I had become deeply involved in helping to run a club for the disabled in Cardiff, raising money by arranging dances, tombolas, etc., which I enjoyed immensely. People would smile at me and say, "Ah, Sally Jane, when *you* ask for money, how can we possibly refuse?" So we did very well!

One evening, a teacher from a local private art college came to the club inquiring if anyone would like to be a model for her art class. Several of us accepted this interesting offer and subsequently had many sessions over a period of nine weeks.

It was always very quiet and relaxed as the students sat painting our portraits, and no hardship for me to sit very still in my wheelchair with my eyes roaming from one to another. Saint Saba came and stood beside me, teaching me further about the aura which I could see plainly around each one. There was a particular young lady whose aura had such bright, beautiful colours which showed her to be a gentle, spiritual person. Weeks later, when my portrait was finished, this lady presented it to me and I was really surprised when I looked at it and saw that she had painted *my* aura all around my head.

This oil painting now hangs in my sanctuary, always a lovely reminder of those nine quiet weeks which enabled Saint Saba to teach me so much more.

From time to time, I had to go back into hospital to have an operation and be put into what is called a retention plaster. This necessitated having a bar fixed between my legs, which was most uncomfortable. Altogether I had this done seven times, the first cut being only a small one, but with each operation the cut became longer. With every operation I would be in hospital for three months, but on returning home again life carried on where I had left off.

Sometimes Mama and I would go for a visit to Auntie Doris. One afternoon Paul brought a young lady – a psychic – home with him to meet me. We talked together and got on splendidly. She said, like so many others: "Sally Jane, you *must* begin to venture out and do something about your gifts. I suggest that you join the Spiritualist movement at the Summer School in Penarth."

She explained that "Summer School" was a place where anyone could go to hear lectures about mediumship, healing, clairvoyance, etc., and to see mediums demonstrating their gifts.

Now up to that time, Mama, my friends and I had always attended a Church of England, sometimes twice on Sundays, and had been brought up with a deeply religious conviction. We were, therefore, rather hesitant about making such a change. Yet I knew something would have to be done to help me to go forward.

However, about that time, I had been invited to visit friends in Grimsby. Mama and Auntie Doris took me to the station to see me off, where special arrangements had been made for me beforehand. Two station staff were going to lift me and my chair up into the carriage.

We waited until it was nearly time for the train to depart, but, alas, nobody came to help me. This meant that I had no alternative but to travel in the guard's van.

The guard, rather a grim-faced fellow, seemed disinclined to talk, and almost grudgingly said, "Good morning, Miss," but I could see he had a heavy weight on his mind.

As it would be a long journey for me, the Red Cross had promised to send someone to see me to the toilet when the train had a long stop at one of the stations. When we arrived at the station concerned, the guard opened up the large van doors, stepped out and walked away. I sat looking out anxiously, waiting to catch sight of the people who were coming to help me. By this time I was feeling very uncomfortable and becoming desperate, but alas, nobody came. Suddenly, Grampy Danter appeared close by, saying, "Don't worry, someone is coming to help you now."

And almost as he spoke, the two young women with whom we had been chatting on the platform before the train left came walking past with children in pushchairs. When they saw me they stopped with a look of surprise on their faces. "What are you doing here?" they exclaimed.

I told them of my predicament. "Oh, come along, we'll take you," they said, and those lovely young women, who had never been used to handling anyone with a disability and in a wheelchair, did just that – and was I grateful!

Even that journey was not without its psychic incident. Soon after the train moved off, I suddenly had a kind of vision, of a tall, thin, young man, sitting in the corner of the guard's van. The poor lad was obviously very mentally-handicapped, as he sat rocking backwards and forwards, like a very young child in great distress.

I looked across at the guard, who had been sitting on a packing case, with eyes lowered and head bowed, shoulders rounded, in a very despondent manner. Of course, he was totally unaware of what I could see, but suddenly stood up and came over to me with such a changed expression on his face.

"You must find it very difficult to travel in the wheelchair, Miss," he said kindly. "Have you still got your parents?"

I told him how Mama and Auntie Doris had seen me off at the station, and that my friends were meeting me at my destination.

"I like to be as independent as possible in case the time comes when I am left without a family," I told him.

At this, the guard poured out his troubles, words coming out fast.

"I've got a different sort of problem that's nearly wearing me out," he said. "My son is almost 20, but his brain never developed and he's just like a small child. I have someone who comes to the house to look after him whilst I'm at work, but all the time I worry so much about what would happen to him if I was taken ill or had an accident. I dread to think of him being taken into an institution."

He had become very agitated so I patted his arm to calm him a little and said gently: "I want to explain something to you. I am a psychic. You probably know what that means. I am able to see things other people do not. In my mind's eye now, I am looking at your son exactly as he is."

As I went on to describe the young man to his father, I could see the spirit forms of the guard's relations gathering around him. They told me to remind him of several private family occasions, and things of which only he could have known. Listening intently, the guard looked at me in utter amazement.

"Good heavens, how on earth can you know that?" he exclaimed. "Well, Miss, if you have got this gift, can you please see into the future and tell me about my boy?" he almost begged.

Grampy Danter told me to tell him that very shortly someone would come into his life, who would care lovingly for his son, and all would be well. When I explained this to the guard, the look of utter relief on his face was wonderful to see. Almost visibly he "shed his load" and smiling with moist eyes, took both my hands and thanked me profusely.

This is one of the lovely aspects of being a medium, to experience the feelings of joy, warmth and happiness, flooding over my body when I have been able to help someone.

*Chapter Eight*

## REJECTION

ON returning home after my short holiday, I was eager to go forward to begin my psychic work. Mama and I again talked about joining the Spiritualist movement. The Orthodox Church we knew taught that there was a "Life Hereafter," but no one within the church could direct anyone further towards a fuller understanding of what that actually meant, or even how it is possible for an especially gifted medium to act as a bridge between this world and the next.

We decided that if I was to do the work for which I had been born, it would be necessary to join people who really understood these things. We went to the summer school and were greeted by a friendly medium called Mrs Simmons. As we chatted, before going to the lecture room, I was thrilled when she took my hands and said, "My goodness, young lady, your psychic gifts are absolutely beaming out of you."

Mrs Simmons then introduced us to some of the top mediums, Gordon Higginson, Jack and Betty Wakeling and others, who were extremely kind, giving me a lot of encouragement and advice.

We watched intently as the mediums demonstrated their various gifts. Afterwards several of them came to talk to us. Unfortunately, though, one or two seemed rather reluctant to enter into conversation, putting up a hostile barrier as they stared at my wheelchair and no warmth came from them to me at all. One lady almost aggressively fired questions at me.

"You're very young to have had much experience," she said. "How long have you sat in a development circle? It takes years you know."

When I replied, "I have never needed to sit in any church circle," she made an impatient scoffing sound and walked away.

Several other mediums were standing in groups, talking together. I overheard one say in a loud whisper, "How on earth does she think she could possibly serve on the rostrum in that wheelchair?"

This infuriated Mama, and upset me terribly, of course, because no one had even seen what I was capable of doing! We went there a few more times, and then decided that although summer school had been interesting, it could not further my development. It did give me, though, a clearer idea of the way things were done in the Spiritualist movement. It also made me realise that when the time came for me really to begin my work, it would need to be done in my own individual way . . . and it was not going to be easy!

Before leaving, Mrs Simmons suggested we should visit a few Spiritualist churches, offering to demonstrate my gifts. This we did, but again we received a mixed reception and nobody invited me to anything. There seemed to be a kind of attitude that because I was in a wheelchair it was not reasonable to suppose that I could possess psychic capabilities – or even an IQ!

"What gives them the right to tell me I will never be able to serve on the rostrum?" I would complain bitterly after such rebuffs. "Does everybody look at disabled people and think they are second class citizens, not at all like themselves?"

Mama had always brought me up to look upon my chair as a great boon, but at times I almost hated it. Then she reminded me that my life would always be a great challenge. Society owed me nothing, but I would be able to give something to society through my God-given gifts.

However, there was one friend of the family, a medium named Mrs Caduggen, who is now in the spirit world. She used to come to church with us, and on our way home would say: "Don't be discouraged by what they say, Little One. Just ignore them. I promise you the right path will open up to show you the way forward; just you wait and see."

It was encouragement such as this which enabled me somehow to keep an optimistic outlook that things would work out if only I could break down the barriers. The man Grampy Danter had promised would help me had not yet come along.

About this time, Mama opened a new hairdressing salon and thought that it would be a good idea if I went there with her each day to work as her receptionist. It would be a completely new experience for me meeting different people and doing a responsible job.

The customers were very friendly, never mentioning my wheelchair or disability. I really enjoyed sitting behind the desk, answering the telephone and booking appointments. One day, though, something rather upsetting happened. Mama came to me and said, "I'll take you to the toilet now, Sally Jane," and proceeded to push me past a young woman who was having her hair brushed out.

The lady said to Mama, as if I were not there, "Don't you find it a terrible burden?" There was a gasp of disapproval from some of the staff. Looking quickly behind me at Mama's face I could see a deep red flush of anger flooding over her, but in a controlled voice she replied: "No, no, not at all. How could someone I love be a burden?" She pushed me quickly through.

Afterwards, seated back behind the desk, when the lady came to me to pay for her shampoo and set, she looked highly embarrassed, hardly being able to look me in the eyes, and said not one word!

Over the years, I learned to build up a strong defence against hurtful and thoughtless remarks. Happily, people today, by means of articles in women's magazines and TV programmes on the subject, have been educated to understand more about the needs of disabled people and many of the old attitudes no longer exist.

Months passed by, and I had celebrated my nineteenth birthday. By this time I had begun gradually to be accepted in a few of the churches, even being invited to give short addresses. Sometimes, after the services, one of the ministers would pat me on the head and say kindly, "Very nicely done, Sally Jane."

But that was as far as they were prepared to go with me – and *still* my psychic gifts were not being used. How often I remembered the experience Mama and I had in the church in Indiana, where a kind of prediction was given to me of what I would have to endure, but still, I never gave up.

On 'bad' days, Grampy Danter would come to calm me, saying gently: "Have patience a little while longer, my Angel. Soon now!"

Meanwhile, many other psychic experiences were happening to me.

Several evenings each week my work at the disabled club continued. There was a nice young man named Ken who came to help. He was a good friend. We got on very well together. Although not psychic, he had a sensitive, caring nature. Somehow there developed between us a kind of telepathy, which caused us a great deal of amusement. For instance, we were always searching our minds for new ways of raising money for the club. Suddenly, perhaps I would get a good idea and could hardly wait to tell him, but at exactly the same moment that I began to speak Ken was telling me *his* great idea that he'd suddenly thought of – both ideas were identical! It also happened many times that when we needed to discuss matters on the telephone both his line and mine would be engaged for ages . . . simply because we were dialling each other at the same time!

Ken and I were taking a Youth Leadership Course when I had to go into a London hospital for another operation, but he promised to come and see me as soon as visitors were allowed.

The night before Mama and I travelled to London I had another psychic experience – and a very frightening one at that. Awakening suddenly from sleep, clairvoyantly I saw Ken enveloped in flames, flinging himself into water. This disturbed me very much.

I told Mama, "I'm sure Ken is in trouble," but with all the hurried activity of getting ready for the journey, then getting settled in a hospital bed, the episode got pushed to the back of my mind.

Next day, the operation was carried out so it was some days later before friends were permitted to visit me. Although I could see the spirit forms of Grampy Danter and Victoria standing by my bed there was no sign of Ken. Nor did he come any day all the next week. There was not even a 'phone call. I became terribly worried and kept remembering my psychic experience.

Previously, Ken had given me his new office telephone number where he worked as a computer programmer, so I asked one of the nurses if she would kindly telephone to see if it was possible to find out what had happened. The nurse came back with grave news – Ken was in hospital after being badly burnt in a terrible accident. They had heard that he kept calling my name when he was delirious and in danger of dying, but no one knew how or where to contact me.

The shock of this did nothing to help my recovery. As I was lying there in great pain and discomfort, fast entering that post-operative state of feeling very sorry for myself, Grampy Danter appeared, bringing a lovely nun to see me, saying: "This is Sister Angelina. She would like to talk with you."

What a lovely young girl she was, so sweet and gentle. Her loving, calming influence soon began to soothe me. Angelina told me about her life, and how she had been killed during the last world war. She had the care of children in an orphanage in France where the bombs were falling all around. She tried to get her charges out, but a bomb fell directly on them and she, and many children, perished.

Angelina told me that later on she would be coming to assist me in my work, and does so now whenever a calming influence is needed for a distressed person, coming to me for healing and help.

So you can see how gradually my lovely "band of helpers," my "guardian angels," began to form. Happily, after several months, Ken recovered.

## Chapter Nine

## THE MAN COMETH!

WHEN I was able to return home again, Mama asked a spiritual healer if he would come and give me treatment.

Several times previously she had requested this of other healers, who upon seeing me realised that my condition was a karmic one, which "must be endured and not cured." Reluctantly, they decided not to take on my case.

We were very grateful indeed, when Kevin came to help. He had not been told of my psychic capability. When I first saw him, I knew by the lovely colours in his aura he was a very genuine and personal person, but that there was much personal grief within him.

Soon after that first healing treatment I kept seeing, clairvoyantly, a pendant on which hung the carved head of Tutankhamun. This puzzled me greatly for it seemed to be totally unconnected with anything in my life, or that of my family. Yet, it kept happening, so one day I told Kevin about it. He gave me an astonished look as he opened the top button of his shirt and drew out a long chain which had been completely hidden from sight. There, dangling before my eyes, was the Tutankhamun pendant I had been seeing for days.

Mama came into the room with a tray of tea. Kevin told her exactly what had happened. She then explained to him all about my psychic capabilities.

Handling me the pendant he said: "This belonged to my wife, Marion, who passed away some months ago. I always like to wear it close to me. I had a wonderful, beautiful experience. Even though it was such a sad, devastating time for me when Marion was dying, I watched in amazement as her spirit arose slowly out of her body. I saw several of her family, who handled her gently until they all disappeared. So I knew she would be well taken care of. Without that memory I wouldn't have been able to carry on."

As I held the pendant in my hands I could feel Marion's spirit body around me very strongly. Gradually she appeared, standing right behind Kevin. As I described her in every detail he was overjoyed. His questions came thick and fast, but I was able to answer each one of them, besides adding many personal remarks from his wife.

All the time Marion's spirit form was with us, the room was filled with the sharp citric aroma of oranges. When I remarked on this, Kevin was most moved as he told us: "When Marion was pregnant she had a strong fancy for oranges all the time. It's amazing how you know about that."

This was one of the many "meetings" he had with his wife, which brought him such comfort and happiness. This made him so grateful that in order to help me go forward I was invited to go with him to one of the local Spiritualist churches where he gave talks on healing and demonstrations.

"Don't worry, Sally Jane. *I'll* see that you that you get your chance!" he told me.

The following Sunday there was I in the church sitting beside Kevin on the rostrum, being invited by the minister to give a demonstration. This I did with complete confidence. Afterwards some members of the congregation came up to me, shook me by the hand and said: "You should have been up there a long, long time ago. We just didn't know how good you were." Had it been possible, I would have been walking on air! But I was most certainly overflowing with happiness. So many people had tried to discourage me and caused me a lot of suffering and frustration because of their rejection, but today all the barriers were broken down. At last I had been accepted – and my work really had begun.

As I looked at Kevin's beaming face, it suddenly dawned on me that Grampy Danter had been so right, for here, indeed, *was* the man he had promised would come along to help me.

After this I was invited to give demonstrations at other churches, and people began seeking my help. Suddenly, because of the nature of my work, my world became filled with troubled people who sought help in various ways. They did not see my wheelchair as being an obstacle at all in my work. With the spirit helpers, I was able to heal, advise and direct them through black periods in their lives.

Being kept so busy every evening soon made me realise that it would not be possible for me to continue helping at the disabled club, so reluctantly I had to hand over the work to someone else. All that I had been able to do for that club was amply repaid for one night just being there saved my life.

There was a delightful young physiotherapist named Sue at the hospital where I had my operations. She had many good qualities, with a gentle manner, and we became great friends. One evening Sue telephoned to ask if I would like to have an evening out with her and some friends, but I had to decline because it was my club night.

"Never mind Sally Jane. We'll arrange something else another time," she said cheerfully.

On her way home from that evening out, Sue took a wrong turning in the dark . . . and drove straight over the side of a deep quarry, being killed instantly. Soon afterwards, however, she came back to me, saying she would like to help with my work. Sue became one of my wonderful band of healers, a strong guide, and uses reflexology when someone needs manipulation of hands or feet, placing her hands over mine and guiding me to the appropriate point so that healing can take place.

*Chapter Ten*

## MAMA GETS MARRIED

SINCE the day when father left, he had not made any contact with us whatsoever. It was now several years since one of his relatives notified us of his death.

The day before my 21st birthday Mama met a charming man named Ivor Watts. They fell in love and married. At last I had a Dad. So began a new chapter in my life.

Any secret thoughts I may have had as to whether he would be able to accept my disability and my psychic gifts were quickly dispelled for he never questioned these things at all, proving him to be a lovely gentle and kind man, one who has loved Mama and I dearly ever since.

"Your gifts obviously come from God and they must be used to help people," Dad would tell me. When his mother, who was in the spirit world, came to me, wanting to give a personal message, his happiness knew no bounds. I described the dear lady. He looked at me in wonder, saying, "That's exactly how your Nana Watts was."

Grampy Danter came to me shortly afterwards and asked me to put a bunch of roses on his grave. He gave me no reason for his request and although I wondered about it, did so next day. In the middle of the following night I awoke and saw Grampy Danter linking arms with Nana Watts, both smiling happily. He said to her, "My 'Little Angel' has put some red roses on my grave just like these," and he placed a similar bouquet in her arms. "It's wonderful, you know," he said, his eyes sparkling. "We have found out that we were together in one of our past lives, and here we are again."

Whenever he came to me after that, Nana Watts was always with him. So at one were they with each other that it was almost like a spiritual marriage. Some times I would see Grandmother Danter standing in the background. She never came forward to speak, but looked perfectly happy with the situation.

Most of the time after an operation I stayed in bed, or in my chair, rarely going into other rooms, but on one occasion when I did venture out and looked into Mama's bedroom where she sat at her dressing-table brushing her hair, I was delighted to see a framed picture of Nana Watts beside her looking exactly as I knew her!

Life went on in a very happy way. I was always busy as more and more people came to me for help, making me feel completely fulfilled. Most of my days there has been pain in parts of my body, but when someone in trouble sat down in front of me, all my discomfort would go, returning only when my work with them was finished.

At this time there were no plans for any further operations, but one night Grampy Danter and Nana Watts stood by my bed and showed me a vision of the Virgin Mother. She looked so beautiful in a long, pale blue dress. On her lovely face there was such a look of compassion. Tears glistened in her eyes as she smiled at me, making me almost transfixed by the sheer wonder of it all.

Grampy Danter said: "My Angel, soon you will have to go into hospital for a more serious operation. There will be others to come, but so as to prepare you, each time this is about to happen we will come to you with this vision of the Holy Mother. This will show you there is nothing to fear, for we will always be with you and all will be well."

Sure enough, three weeks later, the surgeon who had already carried out several operations on my legs contacted Mama to tell her I was now ready to undergo a further one.

So back into hospital I went. As always, when they were wheeling me on a trolley towards the operating theatre, I could see my guardian angels walking beside me. Their presence was so comforting that any fears I may have felt were quickly dispelled and I faced it all with a calm mind. Afterwards, back again in my bed, as I was coming round, there they were again. They had never left me! One would imagine that during these times of intense pain and discomfort all things psychic would be inactive or dulled, but no. Something happened which set things going again in full swing.

Early one morning, just before the day staff were coming on duty, I saw a male nurse come into the ward and start talking to the night nurse, who was just about to leave. Suddenly he looked in my direction, staring hard, and strode quickly over to my bed. He came to an abrupt halt, a look of utter disbelief on his face.

"Good grief!" he exclaimed. "I'd swear I saw four ghosts standing beside you, but now they've disappeared. I've never seen anything like it in my life, Sally Jane."

I laughed aloud at his bewilderment and explained to him that he must be psychic and was not just seeing things. I told him briefly what being psychic meant, and that I was a medium. With a perplexed look on his face he went back to where the other nurse was watching with a very puzzled expression. There was quite a stir of whispered conversation as the day staff entered the ward. One of them giggled uncertainly, while another said: "Don't be daft. You're pulling our legs."

There was one young nurse, though, who stood staring thoughtfully in my direction. That day, she asked me many questions about it all.

Very soon, the hospital "jungle telegraph" had broadcast the news around all the ward – and there were many jokes made about "Sally Jane's ghosts." The next time Phyllis, the hospital physiotherapist, came to give me treatment she pulled the curtains, sat down beside me and said with a somewhat quizzical expression: "What's all this I've been hearing about you? If you really are a medium, Sally Jane, you're just the person I need to talk to for my life is a complete mess and I've been trying to pluck up enough courage to consult a medium for ages."

I told her I would be delighted to help her so she promised to come back when she was off duty. "I'll be looking forward to it," she said as she left.

After visiting hours, Phyllis came back, pulled the curtains for privacy and sat down beside me. Taking both her hands in mine, I studied her aura, and so many things came flooding into my mind. No wonder her life was a mess! With the help of some of my guides, we discussed all the things causing her so much trouble and grief. Several members of her family in the spirit world came to bring words of advice and comfort. Gradually we were able to show her the way through the dark period of her life. All this time, Phyllis sat wide-eyed with amazement, thanking me profusely for giving her such a first-class demonstration of mediumship. She left smiling brightly. Years later, I heard Phyllis had done exceedingly well in her career; her life had turned out to be a very happy one indeed. Once again, I experienced the lovely feeling of contentment, because my work had helped somebody.

When the news of Phyllis' private sitting reached the other nurses many of them came to my bedside for help. Unfortunately, though, being psychic does not automatically mean that one is a happy medium, because there are many times when being able to see ahead can be heartbreaking. For instance, looking around the ward at ladies in the other beds, I could see by their auras the ones who would fully recover and those who would not. It was very sad for me to watch the worried faces of the visitors who came to see these poor patients, knowing as I did, that soon the physical presence of their loved ones would be lost to them forever. Unfortunately, one has to learn to accept these things when one is a medium for it is a life of joy and sorrow.

A few months later, when I was allowed to go home to help my convalescence, we all went for a long weekend to stay at my cousin's 300-year-old hotel in Wales. After a lovely meal we sat talking to some of the other guests in the pleasant lounge bar until it was bedtime. My bedroom was conveniently on the ground floor. After Mama helped me into bed and said goodnight, she left.

I settled back comfortably, going through my absent healing list, which had been growing rapidly, suddenly, over in the corner of the large room, there appeared the spirit form of a very tall, handsome young man. He was dressed in the uniform of a coachman of bygone days. Over this he wore a red cloak. He came towards me, smiling.

"My name is Dowey," he said, going on to tell me that many years ago he had gone out to the hotel stables to saddle a horse, carrying gold sovereigns in his money-belt. Dowey was set upon by robbers, one of whom forced a pistol into his mouth. He fired and killed him outright.

I sensed such a great loneliness within him when he spoke, but he seemed very pleased to have found someone who could see and talk to him.

"My little daughter, Rosemary, died before that happened," he said. "I grieved for her so much when I came here until she found me. I would love you to see her."

Almost as he spoke, Dowey faded gradually from sight and I was left wondering. A few minutes later, he returned bringing with him a pretty little child with fair, curly hair, who stood smiling shyly at me. There they remained for a short time before disappearing.

Next morning, when Mama brought me a cup of coffee, she asked if I had slept well. I told her of my psychic experience. She remarked without surprise, "I had wondered if you would see anything in this old place. Even as we journeyed home, I could feel the presence of Dowey and Rosemary still with me. Mama has occasionally seen them both in my sanctuary.

*Chapter Eleven*

## MAKING HEADWAY

ALL this time Grandma Thomas had been watching with pleasure the way my psychic work had been progressing and would say to me: "Oh yes, we know that your cousins have got their degrees, but you, my lovely, are going far, in a much different way. God has chosen you to do his work for humanity. Many thousands of people will come to you for help."

Of course, Grandma Thomas was very psychic and had many experiences about which she would tell us. I remember the time she went to comfort an old friend, whose husband had just passed away. On entering the house she saw the old gentleman's spirit form standing at the top of the stairs. When she was telling us about it afterwards, it upset her very much, because she had been unable to explain to her friend that the husband was there. Gran knew that the lady did not believe in such things. Thankfully, my work allows me to bring much comfort to ease the great sadness of bereavement.

When, one day, Grandma gently said to me, "Sally Jane, I'm afraid Auntie Doris will not be a long liver." I was appalled at her words. Icy fingers of fear gripped my heart. The very idea of being without my much-loved aunt didn't bear thinking about. Because I knew Grandma Thomas always saw true, the heavy feeling in the pit of my stomach told me there would come a time when my life would be drastically changed and I must begin to prepare for it. Meanwhile, Auntie Doris continued to look the picture of health, full of fun and vitality, so I decided to put the whole idea to the back of my mind and not to worry about it.

My work continued as busily as ever, with more people hearing about my capabilities coming to the house or telephoning to make an appointment for a private sitting. One or two, however, came to me not really for healing or spiritual help, but for an explanation of something strange that had happened to them.

A young girl I knew called Mary arrived at our house one day terribly distressed.

"I had such an eerie dream, Sally Jane, though it seemed more than a dream, because it was so real," she told me. "You remember my brother who died a few years ago. Well, he came and stood beside my bed and seemed to be calling me. It was almost like seeing a ghost. What do you think it can mean?"

I soothed her saying: "Oh, there's really nothing to worry about. He wouldn't have come to hurt you, Mary, only to watch over you and help you in your life."

However, as we talked, I could see Mary's brother standing beside her and knew that it would not be long before she joined him in the spirit world.

Not long afterwards, Mary moved house and would sit outside in the new garden, but because she was in poor health she caught cold. We heard later that Mary had died of pneumonia.

Another young friend called Joan, also confined to a wheelchair, confessed to me her great heartache and loneliness since the recent sudden death of her mother. Tearfully, she said: "Everything is so changed, Sally Jane, that I just can't get over it. Sometimes Mum seems to be so close to me. Yesterday I even imagined that I saw her. Oh, if only things were the way they used to be."

I felt full of sympathy for this girl because she looked so crest-fallen, when there appeared the spirit form of Joan's mother.

"Please say, don't grieve so much," she said. "I will always be near her."

Joan looked at me in wonder when I passed on this message and brightened visibly. However, I could see by the colours in the aura, which were changing to a dark, muddy grey, that before long they would be together again in the next world. Four weeks later she passed on.

Many sceptics cannot accept the idea that their relations are able to return after death. Nevertheless, whether they believe it or not there is always someone from the spirit world with us, even as we sleep, watching over us and helping in many wonderful ways.

In every walk of life there are unhappy people with serious problems, which cannot be solved by doctors or priests. If only they would allow a medium to seek spirit guidance, so much help could be given to them. I have known many who came to my sanctuary weeping in despair and so lonely because they have lost a loved one. With the guides and I working together we are able to prove to them that there is no such thing as the death of the spirit personality, rather a passing into a higher dimension, a spiritual rebirth, where they are as alive as ever they were on earth.

In time, instruction is given to the "new arrivals." They learn it is possible to make contact with those left behind by means of a medium, who acts as a sort of go-between. However, no medium can call up, or summon, a spirit being to bring them back. There is no need!

Most of the time, when a medium is working on the rostrum or at a large demonstration, there are so many people from the next world clamouring around, trying to have messages given to relatives and friends. Of course, it is just not possible in the time allocated, so many people go away disappointed.

The sadness this causes both here and in the next world was clearly shown to me one night after giving a church demonstration. I was sitting quietly at home, meditating, when suddenly the loud pitiful crying of a child filled the room. Clairvoyantly, I could see a curly-haired little boy about four years old, standing beside me, his cheeks flushed and in great distress. I recognised the little chap instantly for he had come to me a few hours earlier when I was on the rostrum. He wanted me to give a message to a lady in the congregation, to be passed on to his mother who was not present.

"Oh dear, Oh dear, whatever is the matter, my darling?" I asked.

"I'm Billy," he sobbed. "I wanted that lady to tell my Mummy that I'm here and she didn't let her know."

At this point he became so agitated that I had to soothe him. "Never mind, if you come with me next Sunday, we'll try again shall we?"

So, the following week, at the beginning of my demonstration, Billy went and stood beside the lady in question. Again I gave her the message to pass on to his mother. On the way home I said to Mama, "I have a feeling that the lady won't do it." And she didn't!

Even though I repeated Billy's message on the following three Sundays, his mother never received it.

It is such a sad thing when people do not feel that they can pass messages to friends and relatives who were not present at the time. Perhaps it is because they think that the recipient would not accept it, through their lack of understanding on the subject. One lady was heard to say, "I just couldn't tell my friend that her husband was there for she doesn't even know that I go to a Spiritualist church."

No doubt that friend would have been only too delighted – and so would Billy's mother. Oh, the pity of it all!

## Chapter Twelve

## MORE PSYCHIC EXPERIENCES

AS the months passed by, there were so many psychic experiences everywhere I went.

One sunny afternoon, soon after I came out of hospital recovering from one of my operations, Auntie Doris took me for a walk in my wheelchair. We were going to look at the shops and then call in at the salon to say hello to Mama.

On our way, we had to pass a large cemetery. Suddenly I was aware of the spirit form of an elderly gentleman walking beside us. He told me of his great love for his grandchildren, and how he could not accept his dying with cancer and leaving them behind.

"It makes me so unhappy because they don't even know that I am here, " he said.

His voice, although sad, seemed to be so calm. I realised he had become earthbound and needed "rescuing" from his present condition. He spoke again and said: "Call me Poppa, my dear. You know, in the spirit world they have told me that the only way to find happiness is to help humanity, so will you let me help you?"

At the salon, Mama greeted us with such sad news. "We've just heard about the terrible Aberfan disaster and the death of all those poor little children," she said with tears in her eyes.

On the way back home, Poppa came to us again, shaking his head sadly as if totally bewildered.

"I just can't understand why things like this happen to innocent children. Wouldn't it have been better to have taken sick people lying near death in hospital?" He disappeared before we could talk further.

One night shortly afterwards, when I was lying in bed, restless with pain, Poppa suddenly appeared and said, "Don't worry, I'll get you out of there."

During my next sessions of physiotherapy I could see him standing nearby, urging me forward with words of encouragement as I struggled to walk. This kind of support really did help.

He comes very often to assist me when there is urgent need for the immediate boosting of a person's morale, and by helping humanity in his own particular way, he is also aiding his own spiritual progression.

Another experience I remember was when we were out for a car ride with friends. They were visiting relations who lived in a lovely farmhouse. When we arrived, everybody except me went into the house. I remained sitting in the car. Suddenly a white haired old gentleman appeared nearby leaning on a shovel. He turned and smiled broadly at me before gradually fading from sight.

Later, when my friends and the farmer came out to the car, I told them what I had seen and asked, "Do you know who that old man might be?"

"Oh, yes," the farmer replied. "You have described my father perfectly. He loved gardening and was a jovial sort of chap, always smiling. It's marvellous to know that he is still around." He sounded quite excited, adding, "I'm going in to tell my family all about it."

Three years later, that farmer's wife passed away. On the several occasions when he and his daughter came to me for a private sitting, I could see his wife standing near him, giving me information about the family, about which I was able to tell them. On one of these visits an old lady also appeared, dressed in a long black gown with a small black bonnet on her head. When I told them that she said she was the farmer's grandma who had lived in the farmhouse many years ago, they were delighted and later brought a photograph of her to show me.

Spirit communicators often bring extra proof of their identity by various means. I remember when a friend came to me in great shock and distress because she had lost her husband in tragic circumstances. Even though he had previously suffered a heart attack, his progress had been so rapid, he was pronounced fit enough to return to work. However, whilst sitting in the doctor's waiting room – he had been asked to go to collect a signing off certificate – he quite suddenly passed away. Someone went to the house to break the news to his wife, and she never saw him there again.

As my friend sat with me in my sanctuary, the room was filled with the aroma of "Old Spice" aftershave. It was so strong it seemed to fill even my mouth, almost choking me. Almost immediately, my friend's husband appeared, and I was able to bring her the comfort she so needed by describing him.

"Oh yes," she said with delight. "That's George, right enough. He always used to smother himself with 'Old Spice.' It filled the whole house."

Then there was the time when two anxious parents came to ask my help in tracing the whereabouts of their wayward daughter, Glenda, who had run away from home. No word had been heard of her since. With the wonderful help of several of my guides we were able to locate and describe the place where the young girl could be found.

Those sad parents went away from my home determined to follow all the spirit-given instructions, went to London, and found their daughter.

Soon afterwards, they brought Glenda to me in the hope that I could "talk some sense" into her, but as she sat in front of me with a sulky and rebellious expression on her face I knew it would not be very long before she ran off again. This happened within a few weeks.

Back came the desperate parents, who really loved Glenda in spite of everything, again asking for help. I willingly gave this, and the girl was found and brought home once again.

Next day, all three came to see me. Glenda was shown into my sanctuary alone, obviously very much against her will. She sat with downcast eyes, morosely silent, as I talked to her. My guides told me what was troubling the girl. When I mentioned one or two of those things she looked up rather startled and sullenly began to mumble replies to my questions. Suddenly, tears welled up in her eyes and the floodgates opened.

When Glenda became more calm, she began to unburden herself to me, pouring out the words quickly, one after the other, telling me all the reasons for running away. It appeared that although it was her dream to go to college and get her degrees, her parents were, in fact, pressing her to do so. She felt she was not brainy enough and would fail, so it seemed the only thing to do was to run away from the situation. She did not want to disappoint her parents by being a failure, and did not even have the confidence to try.

My guides were able to explain that the girl *could* succeed, but if only her heart and soul were put into it. She was capable of achieving all her desires.

Several years later, I heard that Glenda had gone to college, and done extremely well, getting several degrees.

Happy endings like this one are so rewarding for me, for I know how much spirit help changed her whole life.

## Chapter Thirteen

### SPREADING MY WINGS

BECAUSE of my church demonstrations, my work was becoming well known in and around Swansea and Cardiff, but one of our friends, also a medium, said to us: "Sally Jane, I think it is high time you started to advertise in 'Psychic News,' so that people in other parts of the country can benefit from your help."

Before this could happen, though, I knew I would need to be tested by experienced mediums, so it was arranged for Mama and I to stay for a few days at the Arthur Findlay College, at Stansted Hall in Essex. This is a beautiful house standing in its own grounds, where anyone can go for the advancement of psychic studies, by attending lectures and watching demonstrations of healing, psychometry, psychic art, etc. A few days before we were due to leave for Essex I awoke in the night to find Grampy Danter standing beside my bed, showing me a symbolic high, white staircase. Smiling, he said, "You are making your way right to the top of this."

Half asleep as I was, the meaning was not really clear to me, but his words were very comforting when I was feeling just a little apprehensive about the forthcoming visit.

The following night I had two more spirit visitors, one, a young girl called Diane, who Grampy had brought to see me several years earlier. Diane was lovely, with long blonde hair, blue eyes and dressed in a pretty blue corded coat. During her earthly life, she had been a multi-handicapped child, unable to see, hear, speak or walk and yet, in spite of all her disabilities, and trapped within her body, Diane possessed an extremely adult mind, also extra-sensory perception.

Now in her spirit life, not only is she free of all the frustrations she suffered, but all disabilities have left her and Diane is now perfect.

I always find it so wonderful to be able to explain to parents who have lost such a child that their little one in the spirit world will be happy and well looked after by loving relations.

Years ago, Diane had asked Grampy if later she could come and work with me. She has, indeed, proved herself to be a most dedicated worker with psychometry and in healing people with nervous disorders.

On that particular night, though, Diane came to say that she would be helping me at Stansted Hall and that a lady would be bringing a wallet for me to psychometrise.

At Diane's side there appeared another little girl who said that her name was Lisa, and that in her life she had suffered from spina bifida. What a delightful child she was, with very fair hair and the most compassionate eyes I have ever seen in one so young.

"Soon you will be meeting my Mummy," said Lisa. "Please will you tell her you have seen me?"

I promised I would do as she asked, but she gave me no idea where or when this would happen.

Upon our arrival at Stansted Hall, we were introduced to the Principal, Gordon Higginson, mediums Dorothy West and her friend Joyce, who would be testing me, and others.

Later that evening, Mama and I went into the comfortable bedroom which we would be sharing, and after talking for a short time, settled down to sleep. It turned out, though, to be a very restless night indeed, for we were awakened by movements near our bed and could see several spirit forms coming and going. One of them even came and pulled Mama's hair to attract her attention, which didn't please her one little bit!

Next morning, when we inquired whether the old house was haunted, nobody seemed to know anything definite, but we were told that an American lady who had previously stayed there several times refused to sleep in one particular bedroom, because she said that spirit entities disturbed her sleep!

After breakfast, when I was making my way to the testing room where Dorothy and Joyce were waiting to put me through my paces, Frankie, my US Marine guide, walked along beside me, telling me exactly what to expect.

"You will be asked to levitate a table," he said, "and psychometrise a letter. Diane and I will help you."

I went into the room feeling quite confident – and Frankie was proved right. Dorothy asked me to place my hands on a small table and levitate it. Frankie also placed his big hands beside mine, but Dorothy, who could see him, said with a smile: "Would you please take your hands away, young man. We want to see what Sally Jane can do by herself."

I looked at Frankie's face. He was grinning broadly, rather like a naughty schoolboy caught in the act. He stepped back, and I got on with it.

In the dictionary, levitation is defined as "The act of making buoyant or light – the phenomenon of heavy objects being made to float in the air by spiritual agencies."

All the time, out of the corner of my eye, I could see Grampy in the background, smiling, and showing me the symbolic staircase again. Now the meaning of it dawned on me. This testing was like a door opening for me to begin the climb upwards in my profession. I passed this test with flying colours.

The next test was in psychometry, the dictionary meaning of which is, "The occult faculty of divining, by touching an object, the character, personal qualities, etc., of a person who has handled it." For all objects have imprinted upon them hidden vibrations of thoughts and emotions which sensitives are able to pick up. Psychometry is one of the hardest gifts to develop.

Dorothy handed me a letter to be analysed. By holding this in my hands I was able to tell her many things about herself, and described several of her family now in the spirit world. Her verdict was that I had "a remarkable gift." I would be able to help many people. She foresaw that I would go right to the top of the ladder in my profession. Grampy was nodding his head in agreement.

Next day, I was tested for my spiritual healing capabilities. A gentleman was brought into a small ante-room on a kind of stretcher. He had suffered a severe stroke and was partially paralysed, unable to talk, walk or even sit up.

His wife told me that her husband's name was Ted. As I took his hand in mine I saw immediately the spirit form of an elderly lady appear, standing beside him.

"My name is Sally, like yours," she said. "Please tell him that."

So I put my face close to Ted and said: "My name is Sally. Your mother's name was also Sally, wasn't it?"

Ted gave no indication that he had heard me, so I repeated it again and again. We were all watching his face intently and suddenly, to everyone's amazement, his lips began to move, making strange sounds in his effort to speak. At last, out came the name "Sally." I shall always remember his look of sudden delight, as he said it again and again, then "Madge," his wife's name.

Slowly Ted's hand moved in mine. He clung to me as he struggled to raise his shoulder off the stretcher. Gradually Ted sat up for a short time, before falling back with sheer exhaustion. His healing had begun, though, the name Sally being the link unlocking his mind and limbs. I was overjoyed I had been able to help him.

After lunch, we were all shown a very interesting aura machine, and were invited, one by one, to go and stand behind it so we could each have our own aura picture. One of the mediums showed us that mine was by far the strongest aura there. Not only that, the faces of several little spirit children had come out on my reading.

That night, I was in a lot of pain with my back, so Mama slipped into bed beside me to give a little comfort. The warmth of her body against mine seemed to ease me, and we were undisturbed by any mischievous spirit beings. We did, however, both see a beautiful little ballet dancer gracefully flitting across the room, before fading away. We never discovered who she was or why she was there.

Something new and unusual happened to me that same night, though. Mama woke to hear a man's voice very close to her, and to her amazement, realised I had gone into trance . . . and that the voice coming from me was Grampy Danter. He told her that later on I would be able to help her with the further development of her own mediumship. In Mama's early years she possessed a strong psychic gift, but because of the work and stress there had been since I was born, her mediumship had become somewhat blunted.

I do remember one time when Mama slipped into trance, and her Hawaiian guide, Una, spoke to Grandma and I. She told us that soon we would be moving house and that when I was much older an operation would be performed on my spine to straighten it. Both these things came true. I now look forward to the time when Mama reaches her full potential and we will work together.

Next day, some of the visitors attended a lecture for beginners, so Mama and I sat in the lounge, drinking coffee and chatting with several ladies who came to congratulate me on the good results of my tests.

One asked me if I would psychometrise a wallet. Immediately, Diane appeared. Holding the wallet between my hands I could feel her hands resting on top of mine. She explained that the lady was the one whom she had previously mentioned. I told her, "There is money in this wallet which you have never spent."

"Yes, that's quite right," she confirmed. "I just couldn't bring myself to use it."

As she spoke, the spirit form of a man appeared beside her. I described him to her in every detail, explaining that her husband was telling me that he wore a surgical corset. He gave me details of his death, and said he would be with her always. At this, the lady became very emotional, thanking me profusely through her tears for proving that "her Bill" was as alive as he had ever been.

Shortly afterwards, a Mr and Mrs Reed came and sat beside me. Mrs Reed told me that in a case up in her bedroom she had a small oil painting. Could she bring it to me to be psychometrised? I agreed to do so, and off she went to fetch it. Minutes later, she came back into the lounge. This time I saw the spirit form of a grey-clad monk walking beside her.

It was a surprise to me to see that on looking at the portrait, the figure was of a monk who looked exactly like the one standing beside her. Mrs Reed sat down. Taking both her hands in mine, I tuned in. The monk said, "I am her guide, but she is most disappointed, because although we know how well she could do working in trance, as yet she has never been able to surrender herself completely to do this work."

As I listened to what the monk was saying Mrs Reed slumped back gradually against the cushions, as if fast asleep, when suddenly out of her mouth came the familiar voice of Nana Watts. Several other people, seeing what was happening, came over quickly to watch this demonstration of trance mediumship.

One gentleman, I suppose just to test her to see what answers she would give, started asking questions of Nana Watts. "Are you able to tell me where I used to live as a boy?" he queried.

There was a pause. Then came the reply: "Yes. You lived on a canal boat, painted red and white. It had red roses around the windows. Two white horses pulled it along." Amazed, the man confessed this was absolutely correct.

Other people then joined in, asking many questions and receiving answers, very precise, and to the point (which, in life, had always been Nana Watts's way). After a while, she told everyone it was time for her to go, so as not to tire the medium.

Mrs Reed sat up, yawned, and looked around, very surprised to see us all studying her intently – and her husband in tears. The relief when we told her what had taken place was absolute, because she had been trying to go into trance for years, and now, the real work could begin. So grateful were Mr and Mrs Reed, that they gave me a beautiful pendant.

Later in the evening there was to be a full Evening Dress Dinner-Dance. Everyone was looking forward to it. Although I would not be able to join in the dancing, I would thoroughly enjoy the music and watching the other people having a happy time.

Meanwhile, Mama, feeling in need of some fresh air, suggested taking me out for a short walk in the grounds, but as my back had begun to ache again, I preferred to just stay where I was, whilst she went by herself.

Over in the corner of the large room, there was a young girl sitting alone, looking very dejected. It worried me to see her so sad. I wondered what was troubling her.

At my side, appeared the spirit form of one of my guides, Count Sikorsky, who Grampy Danter had brought to me several years ago, when I needed to be very strong about making a decision for my future. He was a Polish nobleman with "blue blood" in his veins. During a war long ago he had fought alongside his two sons. All three of them were killed. The count is a very strong character, with great confidence and strength of purpose. Nowadays, he always comes to help me with people who need to be given this.

"That young lady needs help," he said. "She has a nervous disorder. Her confidence has been shattered by her family, who say continually that her face is so plain no man would want to take her out anywhere, let alone marry her. Come, let us go over and speak."

We went to where the young girl was sitting with bowed head, her hands nervously clasping and unclasping. As we approached, she turned quickly away as if longing to hide.

"Hello," I said cheerfully, "I'm Sally Jane. Isn't this a lovely old house? My mother and I are here for a few days to have my psychic capabilities tested by some of the other mediums."

She looked at me, but remained silent, so I continued talking in a bright, friendly manner.

"We are all looking forward to the dance tonight. Are you?" Her lips trembled visibly. She said bitterly: "No, I'm not going. Everyone will be all dressed up and looking lovely, but how can I with an ugly face like mine even look nice?"

Tears welled up in her eyes, so I broke in quickly.

"Don't be foolish, you've got a pretty little face. If you put on a little make-up, you could look beautiful."

The girl looked up at me, as if unable to believe her ears. At that moment, an elderly spirit lady suddenly appeared beside Count Sikorsky looking on with such love and compassion.

"This is her grandmother," the count told me. "Will you please tell her grand-daughter that she is here. It will help so much."

As I described very gently the lady who had come, dressed in an Indian sari, an expression of wonder came over the girl's face.

"That is my lovely grandmother," she said. "She was born in India."

Tears rolled down her face as she poured out her utter loneliness since the old lady had died.

"Everything used to be perfect while Grandma was there, but now ... " I told her that her grandmother would always be near, and she must never be afraid again.

We talked for a long time and I could see the great tension within her had eased. Count Sikorsky smiled at me and disappeared.

Later, when the dance was in full swing, I was watching everyone around me, when I happened to look up and saw her coming down the wide staircase. Dressed in a beautiful peacock blue gown, there was a gentle smile on her nicely made up face and she walked confidently, glowing with vitality. A young man walked over, took her hand and soon they were swept along to the rhythm of the music. I closed my eyes for a moment, thanking God, for that girl's life had just begun!

Next morning, after breakfast, when we were preparing to leave, Mama went to our bedroom to collect our cases. I was sitting in my wheelchair in the hall waiting for her, when a lady I had not seen before came rushing over to me.

"Oh dear!" she said. "Are you about to leave, or is there time to talk for a few minutes? I'm Lisa's auntie. You know of her don't you?"

It was a surprise! As she sat down beside me, I explained how Lisa had come to me earlier.

"Yes, I know," the young woman went on. "I am a medium too, and my sister, Mary, Lisa's mother, has not stopped grieving since the little girl passed over. No matter how often she is told that there is a spirit world, nothing will convince her. At least she has been persuaded to come here for a few days, hoping that all she sees and hears will open up her mind, but please will you help now?"

Of course, I agreed. As Lisa's auntie beckoned another lady to join us, she said, "Perhaps if you tell Mary that you have seen Lisa it will convince her."

Lisa's mother walked over to us very hesitantly. As we began to talk, Lisa appeared at her side, telling me the things she wanted me to say. With exclamations of amazement, Mary began nodding her head, confirming the truth of what she was being told, and tears began to flow . . . tears of utter happiness and relief because this was all the proof needed to convince her that the little girl was alive and close by.

It was wonderful for me to see that yet again Spirit had been able to bring someone's life out of the darkness and into light.

Just then, Gordon Higginson, the Principal, came and introduced me to a well known spiritual healer, John Cain, who had just arrived, and would be there for a few days giving talks on healing and demonstrations of his wonderful gift.

John ran a large, busy healing centre. I had heard of the marvellous work being done there. So I asked him if he could do anything for me.

He took my hand saying gently: "My dear, I'm sure you know already that as yours is a karmic condition, very little can be done to alter it. Promise me, though, that if your pain becomes too much to bear you will contact me and I will give absent healing at once." In later years, John Cain was true to his word.

## Chapter Fourteen

## MY WORK GOES ON REGARDLESS!

NOT long after returning home from Stansted Hall, the pain in my back worsened so I was taken to be examined again by the same surgeon who had operated on me several times in the past. He decided that yet another one was necessary. Back to the hospital I had to go, by now becoming quite used to the whole routine. Many of the doctors, nurses and other staff were well known to me. Their friendliness and kindness greatly helped my frame of mind.

Before very long I was being pushed along on a trolley through the corridors towards the operating theatre by the same orderly, whose name was Dennis, who had always taken me down for my operations. He would smile at me, and talk in such a nice calming and reassuring manner: "Just take it easy, my little princess (his pet name for me), and I'll have you back in your bed before you know it."

Of course, he was completely unaware of my guardian angels walking beside us! Dennis worked hard and for very long hours in that hospital, but nothing was too much trouble for him. Everyone liked him immensely. Sometimes, during his off-duty periods, he would come and sit beside me, asking if I would tell him more about my psychic work, which by now most people in the hospital accepted.

On one occasion, by holding his watch between my hands, I was able to link up with several of his relations in the spirit world, even his mother, who had passed away at his birth. Dennis was delighted, saying, "What a clever young lady you are, being able to sort out everybody's problems. But why on earth must *you* suffer so much pain? After all, it is God's work you are doing."

I tried often to explain to him about karma, but he seemed unable to grasp it. During one of our chats, Dennis confessed to me he dreaded the thought he might one day suffer the same terrible death that his father had. I was able to tell him with certainty he would not, and that he must not even think about it.

People had noticed, as I had, that lately Dennis seemed rather quiet, most unlike his usual self. I was alarmed to see that his aura, usually so bright and colourful, was now lacking lustre, beginning to break up, turning a dull grey. It was clear his life would not be a long one.

Nevertheless, it was a tremendous shock to us all when we were told that a message had been sent to the hospital, saying that Dennis had been found dead in bed after a cerebral haemorrhage. Everyone was so sad and missed him terribly. It took a long time for us to get over the loss.

I have met so many lovely people in hospital, and a number have come to me for help. Sadly, it is not always realised that even highly skilled members of the medical profession are human too and have normal emotions. They have to put aside their own personal problems, though, when caring for their patients.

A rather timid lady in the next bed said to me, "How can you feel so relaxed when those top surgeons and highly skilled doctors talk to you?"

"I look within them," I replied, "and see only people with similar problems to the rest of us."

One of the very happy things about being a medium is when I am able to assure someone confidently that there is no cause for concern over a loved one who is ill, or that worrying situations will be resolved satisfactorily, for my guides always show me a little way ahead.

A little nurse called Katie, whose mother was a sister, and her father a doctor at the hospital, came to me one day very agitated indeed and said tearfully: "It's no use, Sally Jane. It's becoming impossible for me to carry on in this profession. What shall I do?"

As I looked at the petite figure, standing with bowed head and downcast eyes, Grampy Danter put me in the picture.

Although Katie was well able to cope with everyday work on the wards, she was totally unable to pass her written exams and was afraid to tell her parents for fear of letting them down. I replied: "Katie, my lovely, you are going to have to face this head on. Why don't you go down right now and tell your mother how you feel? It will be quite all right for sure."

She looked at me aghast. "Oh no, that's impossible," said Katie miserably.

"Right then," I told her in a business-like tone, "we'll go together, shall we?"

Katie knew in her heart that this would have to be done eventually, so decided it might just as well be now, and we went to see her mother.

It was not nearly so difficult as Katie had imagined because both her parents accepted the situation. They loved their daughter, and told her that whatever she chose to do in the future they would back her up all the way. Her eyes shone as she kissed me and said, "You were right, Sally Jane!"

Then there was a young nurse called Gaynor, who was making herself ill worrying about possible bad results in her exams.

"I wish your spirits could tell me whether I shall pass or not," she said wistfully.

Grampy Danter and Nana Watts appeared, smiling kindly at the troubled young girl.

"Tell her she will pass," Grampy said. When I did so, Gaynor exclaimed, "Oh, if only it could be true!"

Not many days later, a nurse was pushing me back from the bathroom when we heard a loud shriek, and Gaynor came rushing towards me shouting: "I've passed! I've passed!" Flinging her arms around my neck with tears of joy running down her face she said, "You *were* right, Sally Jane!"

Then there was the time when I was awakened during the night by the sound of many comings and goings, and of whispering voices. One of the nurses, seeing me awake, came over and said that a young girl had been brought in, close to death, after a suicide attempt, so the doctors had been working very hard to save her life.

Early in the morning, young Dr John, an extremely kind and sensitive young man who would often come and sit beside me during his coffee break, walked over to my bed, and sat down wearily.

"It's ironic, Sally Jane," he said. "Here you are struggling to hold on to life – and there is that young girl doing her best to take hers. I don't think we will be able to save her."

He looked absolutely defeated as he sat with his head in his hands. Angelina, my lovely spirit nun, came and said gently, "Tell him that the young girl *will* live." So I did.

"Is this one of your spirit messages, Sally?" Dr John asked.

I nodded in agreement and he seemed to brighten visibly. Dr John walked away, saying how welcome the news was. The young girl recovered completely – and I knew that the shock of the experience would prevent her from ever trying it again.

Several beds away from me there was a Greek lady, whose name was Anna. After her operation she lay restlessly twisting and turning, muttering incoherently in her native tongue, which the nurses found it almost impossible to understand.

However, after several days when Anna was recovering well, she managed somehow by frantic gesticulations to make it clear that she wanted to be brought over to my bedside. Excitedly Anna grasped my hands.

"You are one of 'us,' my beautiful. You can 'see' and 'hear.' Your gift will be known to people all over the world."

Before I could thank her for telling me this, she went on quickly, asking, "Who is the nice gentleman standing beside you with white hair and very blue eyes?"

Of course, she could see Grampy Danter, which pleased me no end because Anna and Mrs Caddogan were the only two mediums who had ever described him to me!

We talked together until the nurse brought our tea. Then, staff nurse walked over to us and said, "How is it that you can understand what she is saying when everything is 'Greek to us'?"

I explained that because both Anna and I had a psychic gift, this somehow gave us a certain compatibility.

At this, Staff Nurse O'Malley looked at me with great interest because, being new at the hospital, she had not heard about my psychic capabilities.

"Really," she said. "Well, I wonder if you could help me? I just can't make up my mind whether to go back to Northern Ireland or stay in England."

With help from my guides I was able to advise her that, without doubt, she should stay in England and would go far in her profession.

On some occasions, though, being able to see ahead can be rather distressing for me, especially when it is a situation where I must not divulge what I have seen.

For instance, a lady called Mary was brought into the ward, and put in a bed quite near mine. As I looked at her, I could see she was very, very depressed. At visiting time, Mama and I could not help overhearing a very heated argument between Mary and her visitors, a much younger woman and a man. Suddenly, the lady got up abruptly from her seat and with a flushed face and streaming tears rushed past us and out of the ward, followed quickly by the young man.

We were very concerned to see poor Mary covering her face, sobbing her heart out. A nurse went to her and pulled the curtains around the bed.

Next day, looking across at the still very distressed lady, we could see that her aura had changed greatly, the colours being very dull, turning to dark grey. It was obvious what that meant.

After lunch, I asked the nurse if she could push me in my chair to Mary's bedside "Just to try to cheer her up."

"That'll take some doing, love," she whispered. "We've been trying to do that all morning, but she just won't tell us what is wrong."

Mary lay with closed eyes, breathing very jerkily. I patted her hand gently and said softly, "What is troubling you, my lovely?"

She opened her eyes, stared up at me for a moment, then struggled up on to one elbow. Putting her arm around me, she cried out broken-heartedly, "They don't want me; nobody wants me."

Gradually, it all poured out. Apparently, because the family felt they would not be able to cope at home with their mother's illness, they had suggested for her sake it would be a good idea if she were to go into a nursing home. Mary felt as if she was being abandoned and unloved, and was in no mood to listen to reason.

She was becoming more hysterical, so I called the nurse, who gave Mary a sedative before wheeling me back to my bed. That night I lay awake, wishing so much that somehow it would be possible for me to advise Mary's son and daughter to make peace with their mother, because it would be the last chance they would get. Neither of them came back again. Next day Mary was moved to a convalescent home. However, it was not long before she was back in the hospital where she passed away, her illness accelerated by her feelings of being unloved and unwanted.

When the young daughter came to collect her mother's few belongings, she came over to me and confessed tearfully: "I feel so terribly guilty, just as if we caused mum's death. We had no idea she was so ill, but honestly we loved her very much and she knew that. We just couldn't make her understand, though, that it would have been impossible for us to look after her at home. I'm out at work all day."

She turned, and walked away. I felt so sad as I watched her crestfallen figure leaving the ward. Oh, the importance of love in all our lives!

Towards the end of that time in hospital, the young orderly, named

Henry, the man who had previously seen my guardian angels standing close to me in the ward, came and sat down beside my bed.

"You know, Sally Jane," he said reflectively, "since seeing your ghosts I have seen several others in various places. There is no one else to talk to about it, so when you are back home would you let me visit and explain it all to me? I mean, what does a medium do exactly?"

It was obvious Henry had psychic capabilities which needed developing. Being so eager to learn about himself, I promised to help.

After he had left me, the ward became quiet, with everybody settling down for the night. I lay pondering just how many people like Henry there must be in the world, psychic, and yet completely puzzled by it all, terrified of confiding in anybody for fear of being looked on as being crazy. Next day, something happened which seemed to confirm my thoughts.

At the far end of the ward a patient was regularly visited by her sister and five-year-old niece. That afternoon, the nurse brought the young mother and little daughter to see me.

"Sally Jane," she said, "this is Mrs Bennett and Tracy. I've told them that you will be able to help with a problem."

Mrs Bennett looked rather ill at ease, but sat down beside me, pulling Tracy on to her lap.

"I hope you don't mind doing this, but I'm at my wit's end with young Tracy," she admitted. "Her dad and I are worried to death. She keeps insisting she sees my mother in the house and talks to her frequently, but mum died a year ago. It's uncanny. We wonder if she needs to see a psychiatrist."

Tracy broke in petulantly, insisting, "I *do* see granma, mummy. She *does* talk to me."

I smiled at the angry, flushed little face. "Look hard at me sweetheart, and tell me want you see."

"Pretty colours all around you, and white," Tracy said without hesitation. Of course, she was seeing my aura. As she spoke, the spirit form of a lady appeared, standing behind them.

"It is quite true," she told me. My grand-daughter has the gift. We know that in the future she will be able to help many people, as you yourself do. Somehow my daughter must be made to understand there is nothing wrong with the child. Please try to explain to her."

I knew without a doubt this is what I must do, so offered to explain it all to Mrs Bennett if she would like to come to my home.

That night Saint Saba came to me just as I was about to drop off to sleep.

"My child," he said. "The young man, Henry, will become the first of many of your students in the future. You will instruct them in all I have taught you; this is the work you were born to do."

Of course, as always, Saint Saba has been proved right, for nowadays I have many students in various stages of development, all being trained by means of tape recordings, telephone conversations, and privately in my home. Each one receives personal attention. I take great pleasure in watching their progress.

Incidentally, when I went into hospital in more recent years and was being pushed along the familiar corridor towards the operating theatre by a new orderly, it made me happy to see Dennis in his white coat, smiling down at me in his usual way, as he walked beside the trolley with my guardian angels.

## Chapter Fifteen

## DARK DAYS

TOWARDS the end of that three-month stay in hospital, I was so looking forward to going home when something happened which cast a dark shadow over my feelings of happy excitement.

Early in the morning, before the usual activity in the ward began, Saint Saba appeared, a lonely figure standing on a large, jagged rock rising out of a turbulent sea. Everywhere there was darkness: angry waves pounded against the slippery sides, threatening to engulf him. He stood his ground, silent, looking at me with such a sad, compassionate expression that conveyed to me more than words could possibly have done, This was his way of preparing me for a dark period in my life which was soon to begin.

After the vision faded, I was left apprehensive, wondering what on earth was about to happen, when the day staff came on duty. Nurses began rousing the patients in order to give them a wash before breakfast.

As the day wore on, I could not shake off a terrible feeling of foreboding. Therefore, when the bad news came, I had been expecting something unpleasant, so was almost prepared for it.

Just after lunch, a nurse came to me, saying: "Sally Jane, I'm taking you down to matron's office. Your mother has telephoned and is waiting to speak to you."

My heat sank. All the way there, I most certainly knew what it meant to have butterflies in my stomach.

I picked up the telephone and heard Mama saying in what I knew to be her forced brightness voice, "Now, don't worry, love, but your Dadda has been taken ill, and is in hospital."

My questions rushed at her. "What is the matter with him, Mama? When did it happen? What do the doctors tell you about his condition?"

Mama did her best to calm me, and said: "You will be coming home tomorrow. We'll go and see him then." She followed this up with: "You'll never guess what else happened, Sally Jane. Your Uncle Arthur has been taken into the same hospital so we will be able to see them both together."

On the way back to the ward, my thoughts were racing. Is this what Saint Saba had meant? Did all the darkness around him mean that both my lovely Dadda and uncle were about to pass into the spirit world? Oh, how I prayed not!

Next day, after being released from hospital, Mama and I went home, had a hurried lunch, then set off to see Dadda and uncle. We left my wheelchair outside in the lobby so I went clattering up the ward in my calipers and walking aid as fast as I could to reach Dadda's bedside. As soon as we saw him, we knew he was very ill indeed. He lay back against his pillows, gaunt and pale, and seemed hardly able to recognise us.

We also found Uncle Arthur in a very poor condition. The way he tried to struggle up to kiss me touched me so much. Beside the bed were Nana Watts and Saint Saba, who told me that uncle would soon be entering the world of spirit. I didn't mention this to Mama since things were bad enough as it was.

However, after several terrible weeks, knowing that Dadda was suffering so much, Saint Saba took me one night, during my sleep, astral travelling to the hospital. I remember it all so clearly, seeing Dadda lying so still. I took his hand and called his name time after time before finding myself back in my bed.

Happily, Dadda came out of the coma into which he had slipped and gradually recovered. Later, when back home with us, he began telling everyone about the strange experience during the very worst time of his illness.

"I felt so terribly ill," he said, "and began drifting off into a lovely peaceful sleep. All I wanted to do was to float away from the pain. All around me there appeared to be many pairs of hands supporting and guiding my weightless body. I was just happy to go wherever they took me. Suddenly, I was startled by the metallic sound of Sally Jane's callipers and crutches, clink-clanking towards me, and heard her voice calling me urgently, again and again, getting louder and louder. She was pulling at my hand. Suddenly, I felt a kind of jolt and there I was, as before, back in this world. There is no doubt whatever that Sally Jane brought me back from the very brink of death."

Of course, this was a perfect example of what can happen during an out-of-body-experience. It was so wonderful for me to know that in this way I had saved Dad's life.

Uncle Arthur seemed to make good progress and came to see us when he left hospital, but sadly died suddenly a short time later.

Again Saint Saba was right in what he had told me. I wondered after the worrying events of the past month, if this was to be the end of the darkness, yet something deep inside me told me otherwise.

With Dadda back home again and in much better health I gratefully accepted Auntie Doris' invitation for me to stay with her and my two cousins for a week. Mama never had any qualms about leaving me there. Auntie Doris was well able to cope with all my needs. We always had a lot of fun together.

As always, they made up a bed for me downstairs in the front room. During the second night there, I was awakened by the presence of my grandfather who showed me a future vision of Auntie Doris lying in a hospital bed. He told me she would become very ill.

I couldn't understand this at all, because there was no one so healthy and full of life as she. But I also remembered Grandma Thomas saying she would not be a "long liver." Once again, the very thought of it made my blood run cold.

Early next day some friends of mine who lived in Dover telephoned to ask if I would like to stay with them after my week with Auntie Doris. One of them was a nurse used to caring for disabled people, so it pleased me no end to accept the invitation. I needed a short break to recharge my batteries after recent draining events and knew that I would restart my work fully refreshed.

In Dover, one of my friends was pushing me along by the sea in my wheelchair whilst three others walked along beside us. We were all chatting happily together enjoying the sea air and the sunshine when quite suddenly a strong feeling of agitation came over me and I experienced a very intense psychic knowing that all was not well with my aunt. Seeing my agitation, one friend said in alarm: "Whatever is the matter, Sally Jane? You have gone so pale. Do you feel ill?"

"Please get me to a telephone quickly," I begged. They rushed me along to the nearest phone box.

The news from Mama was not at all good, for Auntie Doris had suddenly been taken seriously ill with high blood pressure. This proved to be the start of much suffering for her.

Naturally, I travelled back home straightaway, my heart very heavy indeed, and found everyone else there similarly distraught. Every time we visited auntie in hospital I studied her aura, but did not want to believe what it showed.

However, after several weeks she recovered sufficiently to be allowed home and Mama found a healer to treat her. After seeing her, he reported to us that he was very sorry, but he could see spirit people beginning to gather around waiting to "help her over." Even with this, we would not accept what we had been told, and deluded ourselves that it just couldn't be true because she was so strong and would surely get over the illness. Sadly, however, after a few weeks Auntie Doris had to be taken back to hospital where she lingered for a short time before passing away.

Her death completely shattered us all. For me, in particular, a lovely secure and comfortable part of life seemed to have been wrenched away. We all felt great sadness, none of us wanting to eat or even speak. The atmosphere in the house was very heavy.

Even though we all knew so well that Auntie Doris would be out of pain now, and in a far better place, the loss of her physical presence was unbearable. No longer could we pick up the 'phone and hear her cheerful voice as we had done for so long. Gone was her support, understanding and above all, love.

During all this family sadness, people kept telephoning me for private sittings and calling at my house. With a great effort I managed to push away my personal grief to do God's work and never turned anyone away. Having experienced the loss of such a loved one, I found that it showed me exactly what people were feeling when they came in distress, hoping to be reunited with someone they had lost.

At night I cried out to Grampy and Saint Saba, asking, "Why couldn't I have died first?"

Saint Saba looked at me so kindly and said gently, "Because, my child, there is much work for you still to do. It is necessary for you to have all these emotions so you will have complete understanding for others. It is part of your development. But, as always, we will be near."

When I asked him if this sadness was to be the end of the dark days he made no reply before disappearing.

A friend called at the house to offer her condolences, and said to me, "I honestly don't know how you can carry on with your psychic work when your family is having so much trouble."

I tried to explain to her that my work is something I have to do no matter what.

Very soon I was able to bring great joy to two people. Mr and Mrs Davis came in great distress because they had lost their daughter. They sat down in my sanctuary and handed me a ring which had belonged to her. Immediately the spirit form of a young girl with dark hair, wearing red jeans and a white blouse, appeared in the room. She told me she had been driving her Mini. For a split second, as she changed her cassette, she took her eyes off the road, crashing into another car which killed her instantly. The extra sad part was that her parents had been following her in their car a short way behind, going home after buying their daughter a special present for passing her exams. They had the terrible experience of seeing her killed right in front of them.

"Mum has kept everything in my room as it was," the girl told me.

As I was relating all this to the parents, the father was so overcome with emotion that he got up and left the room for a while. When he returned he apologised and said: "We have been to several other mediums, but not one of them has been able to bring our daughter back in such detail. This has made us very happy."

It also makes me so very happy that with the wonderful help of my guides I am able to do this for people. To see the change in them as they leave my sanctuary is remarkable. I thank God for my psychic gifts.

Just as I was beginning to feel that we had seen the last of our troubles we began to notice that Grandma Thomas was no longer her usual self, but we put it down to the fact that she was missing her daughter, Doris, very badly. After being so used to seeing Nanna always bustling about in her business-like way caring for everybody, it seemed so strange and sad to see her just sitting quietly with her eyes closed, sighing frequently and speaking little.

We were very concerned. One afternoon, when I was taking a break from taped readings, I made my way in my wheelchair to the living room and saw Nanna in there alone. I almost cried out "Oh, God, no!" for her aura, usually so beautifully colourful, was now a dull, murky grey. She opened her eyes and said quietly: "Ah yes, my lovely, you know, don't you, but don't fret. I am really looking forward to going to your Auntie Doris, your uncle and so many of my family. No tears must be shed over me. Promise that. For you know how things will be for me. I really am tired now, but remember, I shall always be around. Never fear!"

Grandma Thomas told me many times about her son killed in the war. Everybody knew his death had hit her very hard. Grandma never really got over it. She would also often speak of her lovely sister, Polly, a beautiful young woman with auburn hair, blue eyes and a serene nature. Auntie Polly passed away when she was 27. She comes to me now, working as a guide. A psychic artist once drew a sketch of her when I was giving a demonstration.

Several weeks later, Grandma was taken into hospital where she passed away quickly, aged 88. So ended the earthly life of a wonderful lady, whose strength of character had helped to mould us into the people we are today. She was always supportive and loving, never afraid of hard work. Grandma had borne and raised three children and also adopted a little girl, an unwanted coloured child, with dark curly hair and big, soulful brown eyes. This little girl became my Auntie Gladys with whom we stayed during our visit to America.

Grandma Thomas' death, exactly one month after that of Auntie Doris, made us sad beyond belief. It was, indeed, the end of an era for us. We knew that life could never be the same again. Mercifully, I still had my work so my days were filled with helping people, many even more distressed than ourselves.

At night, I would lie in bed and think, "Well, surely this must be the end of all the darkness." But no, there was another terrible family tragedy to come.

My mother's cousins decided to go strawberry-picking on a lovely summer's day so they set off, each with her husband, to enjoy the fresh air and have a nice peaceful time. As they were walking down a country lane, along came a van being driven dangerously fast by a 16-year-old youth, who had stolen it for a joy ride. On a sharp bend in the road he completely lost control and ploughed into them, killing all four instantly.

So you can see that being a medium and having wonderful guides in no way shields me from heartbreak. But having experienced it all, my character has been strengthened and given me a deep, deep compassion for others.

## Chapter Sixteen

## HAPPIER TIMES

I FEEL very strongly that no matter what befalls us in our life we simply must *not* crumble under it. Life must go on somehow; we need to take up any new challenge which presents itself. Luckily, as far as I was concerned, one soon did, which helped to lift my feelings of depression after all my personal grief.

Several times a week, I had to go to the hospital for more physiotherapy. Everyone there was talking about the urgent need for funds to purchase more hydraulic equipment to be used for raising and lowering patients into the swimming pool. It was decided that several of us would take part in a sponsored wheelchair push . . . all the way to Cardiff.

Each of us had a partner to help us up and down kerbs as we slowly made our way along the roads. It was quite an effort, but very exciting as we covered the miles. People cheered us on, and a friendly policeman helped to ease my wheelchair over a very awkward kerb.

When it was all over we were very tired, but so pleased to have achieved our goal, and the equipment was bought!

Soon another happy occasion came my way. The parents of a friend of mine were having a dinner-dance in a large hotel to celebrate their daughter's 21st birthday. We were all invited.

Oh, the excitement when Mama took me to buy my evening dress! It was made of Chinese silk and had a lovely flowery pattern. Of course, it was never possible for me actually to dance on these occasions but I always enjoyed just sitting at a table watching all the people and listening to the music.

I remember, several years previously, going with friends to another dance when they helped me to walk to a table and hid my walking-aid under the long table cloth. When everyone else was on the dance floor, a very nice young man, whom I had noticed kept looking at me, came over and began to chat, asking if I would like to dance. I thanked him, but made the excuse that it was rather too warm for me. Still he persisted, until at last I lifted the corner of the cloth so he could see the real reason for my refusal. The poor young man looked so embarrassed and full of apologies went away.

So when we received the invitation to this dance, Dadda was determined I should have the pleasure of being on a dance floor just like everyone else. Happily, after my last operation and lots of physiotherapy, I was able to stand upright with the support of my walking aids.

Dadda had a good idea. Helping me up out of my wheelchair, he put his arms around me as if he were a dancing partner, saying, "Put your feet on top of mine."

Fortunately, I was slightly built, but nevertheless it must have been painful for him after a while as we practised "dancing" this way as we did for a few days before the dance. This delighted Mama so much that she took photographs of us.

When the great night arrived, it was hard to describe my feelings of exhuberance and achievement as Dadda and I moved across the dance floor with the other dancers!

Next day, my work continued as usual. By now, so many people were telephoning or writing to me for private sittings that I was kept very busy indeed. Letters came from all parts of the world, so I began collecting all the stamps from them for charity.

A good friend of mine, a nurse, invited me to stay with her for a few days. Mama and Dadda always encouraged me to do this to help me to be more independent, and as a complete break, or so they thought, from my work and all things psychic, but it didn't work out that way!

I was taken in my wheelchair to see the house where William Shakespeare had lived – and what vibrations there were in that place. We walked past the Shakespeare Memorial Theatre. Afterwards, my friends and I found a beautiful spot by the river under a weeping willow tree. There we sat quietly, enjoying the sunshine and the tranquillity.

Suddenly, I saw the spirit form of a lovely young woman sitting nearby. She had long auburn hair and dark eyes. She wore a cream dress and large hat, and had a parasol, but she looked so very sad. Clairvoyantly, I asked her if there was anything I could do to help. She looked at me with such a troubled expression.

"My name is Marguerite," she said, going on to explain that before she had died of tuberculosis her parents always brought her to this spot, which she loved, to take the air.

It was obvious she was an earthbound spirit being, one reluctant to leave the conditions where she had felt so happy and secure.

Before we could speak any more, I felt someone shaking my arm gently, asking: "Are you with us, Sally Jane? We've been asking you what we should all do later on this evening."

One of my friends was looking hard at me, and said: "You've been away. Have you been seeing things that we can't? Well, now that you are back with us again, we can make a decision." Everyone laughed.

All the way home I could sense Marguerite close beside my wheelchair as we walked along. She seemed loathe to leave someone she had found, at last, who could communicate with her.

Back home again, Marguerite kept appearing to me in my sanctuary, and I was able to rescue her.

One afternoon, during my meditation, she appeared smiling happily at me and whispered "Goodbye" before fading slowly from sight. She has never been back. I guess that peace and contentment has come to her in the spirit world.

I can honestly say that in spite of my disability, apart from several bleak, dark periods, my life has been a happy one. I have enjoyed all the various experiences which came my way – between operations.

One such happy time happened some years ago when I was invited with other disabled people, accompanied by doctors, nurses and welfare workers, to go by coach to France and Belgium on a working holiday. The purpose was to meet other disabled people and have discussion groups to find out how they were cared for in their respective countries. We went from Dover by ferry. Everyone there was eager to help us in every way.

In Belgium, however, we were surprised to find that few disabled people ventured far from their homes because they found great difficulty in getting about on the streets or public transport. One of my friends, also wheelchair-bound, and I decided that it would be fun to go for a tram ride, but when one came along the step into it was so high off the ground that it was impossible for us to be lifted up. We were very disappointed, but, of course, have a similar difficulty with buses in our own country. I find that the only way to travel short distances is by car or taxi.

On the trip was my friend Alex (he is able-bodied), there to help with wheelchairs. One afternoon, he took me to the Canadian and British Cemetery because I wanted to look for my uncle's grave. As Alex pushed me along among the gravestones, suddenly a man's voice called my name loudly.

"What are you doing here, Sally Jane?" he asked. "This is Uncle George. You shouldn't spend time looking for me in a sad place like this. Go back and enjoy yourself! You must surely know that I'm not far away, wherever you may be."

At this point, Alex broke in, somewhat startled. "I heard somebody calling your name. Yet there is no one around. Who was it, Sally Jane?"

A few people on this trip knew about my psychic gifts, but not Alex, so I tried to explain about myself. Whilst talking, it was plain to see he was finding the whole idea of this new revelation about me very difficult to accept. This saddened me, because up until that time we had got along so well together and liked each other a lot.

In the past, though, there had been a few other young men of whom I had become very fond and they all reacted in a similar way on discovering this "difference" about me. One of them seemed to accept my mediumship, but said, "You have wonderful psychic gifts, but are so busy I couldn't cope with having to share you with all the people who come for help."

Always when it came to the point where they wanted to become serious, it was plain to me that my work was – and always would be – the most important thing in my life, so I needed great strength of mind to make sacrifices which I have never regretted.

Most of the French and Belgium people were very helpful, but as in all walks of life there were exceptions. One or two turned their faces away or crossed over to the other side of the road when they saw us coming. At one restaurant we were asked to leave because of our wheelchairs, which outraged my colleagues and caused quite a fuss. This sort of thing has happened to me in our country, but over the years I have become immune to such incidents and do not allow them to upset me, not visibly anyway.

Between our working periods we went out and about, thoroughly enjoying seeing all the sights. In one park there were some really beautiful fountains, the water rising and falling together as they responded to the sound of music. Quite amazing!

In Bruges we visited an orphanage run by nuns to see how disabled children are trained. We watched enthralled as elderly ladies with their veined old hands moved so rapidly to produce the most beautiful lace. One poor little poppet was so badly disabled she was hardly able to hold the bobbins yet persistently struggled on. A nun came over to us and said, "We work very hard to train the children so that when they leave us it will be far better for them to fend for themselves."

My heart went out to those children, knowing that as orphans they had never experienced family life or parental love, even though they were being cared for so well.

In Paris, Angelina came to me and, unbeknown to my friends, was able to draw my attention to many extra interesting places and things, but as always, wherever I went there were more psychic experiences.

We were all sitting, relaxing and chatting happily in the hotel lounge with my friend Francoise in her wheelchair close beside me. She was such good company, a bright, happy young woman, who, though unable to walk, had a remarkably keen brain. In fact, she was the very first disabled teacher to be accepted at a school for infants.

"My electric wheelchair seems not to bother the little ones at all," she told me, "but on the first occasion I had to meet parents I felt their eyes ranging incredulously over me as if they wondered how I was able to be in such a responsible position of teaching their children."

Unfortunately, I know exactly how that feels, for it happened to me many times in those early days when struggling for recognition. We do need to put it across to people what we can achieve.

Sitting in those pleasant hotel surroundings, quite suddenly the spirit form of a very attractive young woman appeared to me. She was attired in a lovely black, long-sleeved dress. The spirit visitor had blonde hair and blue eyes, and was slim and vivacious. Giggling, she said: "My name is Evette. I'm a 'lady of the night,' a prostitute."

Clairvoyantly, I asked if there was any way to help her. She then told me how many years ago she was murdered at the very site on which the hotel had been built. Evette was just one of many hundreds of earthbound spirit entities I have encountered so, closing my eyes, I mentally went through all the stages necessary to rescue her.

I then became aware of Francoise gently saying to me: "Are you awake, Sally Jane? We didn't want to disturb your cat nap, but it's time to go into dinner now."

During out next discussion group, one of the Belgian psychologists asked us many questions in a rather abrupt manner. When it was being

debated as to whether people born with severe disablement should be
sent from an early age into an institution, he fired a question at me,
asking, "Well, what would you do if you had a disabled child?"

Without hesitation I replied: "Love it. Above all else, bring it up and
educate it, and make sure it was not disadvantaged in any way. Help
would be brought in when necessary. I would make it my responsibility
completely to bring out all the talents and capabilities the child may
have."

"So you would not place it in an institution?" he persisted.

"No!" I replied. "Definitely not."

He shrugged his disagreement at my reply and went across to one of
the able-bodied helpers. "Well, what would you do?" he asked.

"Exactly the same thing," she replied promptly. I could see that
several of the group were becoming angry at the psychologist's
aggressive manner as he left us in no doubt that he considered us all
wrong to make such a decision.

Saint Saba came close to me and said, "Now, my child, ask him
what he would do in that situation."

As I asked the rather hostile young man the question, he blushed a
little and his dark eyes stared coldly at me. He stammered as he
replied, "Well, it would all depend on if I felt that I could handle it."

After the discussion had ended he came over to me. I could see that
he had mentally left off his professional white coat approach and was
now prepared to talk in a more humane manner.

"My, my, young lady," he said wryly. "You took me aback when you
asked me that question for I'd never really thought about it before."

I asked, "What makes you think we would want to put any disabled
child of ours into an institution?"

"Because most people do," he said.

I continued: "Well, there is a moral issue here, isn't there? When two
people bring a child into the world it is entirely their responsibility to
bring it up, not society's. Parents have so much to offer. Accept all the
help possible, yes, but never abandon one's flesh and blood."

At this, his attitude seemed to change. "I quite agree," he said, "but
there are not many people who are strong enough to face it all."

Saint Saba told me, "That young man has had to harden his heart
because of all the heartbreak he has seen."

Later, when we were all visiting a museum and were shown
"Madam Guillotine," my blood ran cold as I saw the spirit form of a

young Frenchman of about 25 having his head cut off. One of the doctors who stood nearby looked anxiously at me, and said: "Are you all right, Sally Jane? You look so pale. Knowing about your psychic gifts, have you seen something?"

"Yes," I said, "but I'd rather not talk about it." This was not the end of the matter. Next day we visited a large fun fair. I could see Grampy Danter walking along beside me looking very happy, back in the environment he knew so well, with all the different rides and amusements. One of the young male helpers offered to go on the Big Dipper with me when he heard me say how much I'd like to, even though he looked dubious as he suggested it. However, on we went. I found it most exciting and exhilarating, but when it was over, thought that I'd like to have another go. Glancing at the face of my companion I could see it was absolutely green. It was then he told me of his fear of heights, explaining he had only come with me because I could have been frightened up there.

One of the other helpers came over, offering to take me up again, but suddenly a psychic warning came to me from Grampy Danter that something would go wrong with the machinery, but nobody heeded me. My friends and I just watched as the ride started off. Suddenly, there was a loud bang and the ride shuddered to a halt, leaving the people high up in the air, screaming for help. On the ground, everybody was dashing about until mechanics came to carry out the repairs. For me, it was yet another example of how a psychic warning had saved me from danger in the past.

On the morning of our departure back home we all sat waiting in the coach when suddenly the earthbound young Frenchman I had seen on the guillotine appeared to me again. It was clear to me he badly needed to be rescued so closing my eyes I did all that was necessary to release his troubled soul.

Friends in the coach, seeing me slumped in my seat looking so pale, thought I had fainted and became very concerned. They were very relieved when the colour returned to my cheeks and I seemed to be recovered. To me, rescuing that poor young man was very rewarding.

## Chapter Seventeen

## 'RESCUE' WORK

AS I have several times mentioned "rescuing" earthbound spirit beings, for those people who do not know what is meant by this, I will explain as simply as possible, but it is such a complex subject an entire book could be written about this alone.

Rescuing wandering spirit personalties is a speciality of my work which I do gladly, but admit that it is not for the faint-hearted. A medium must be very strong minded, unafraid and full of love and compassion for those souls who are "tied" to their earthly conditions from which they cannot or will not break free. It takes time, patience and prayer, but there are far too few mediums who are prepared to do this work.

When there is a spirit entity badly in need of my help, Grampy Danter and Saint Saba come to me late at night, when the house is quiet, without the disturbing sounds of traffic, telephone or TV. These peaceful conditions are essential, for sudden loud noises could injure a medium who is not sufficiently spirit protected. Of course, with two of my guardian angels watching over me I am never afraid, even when encountering a somewhat violent personality.

First of all, I go into trance so that my own spirit will leave my body temporarily and be free to do what must be done.

Unfortunately, when a person passes over suddenly in a car accident, or by another person's hand, they just do not understand what has happened to them. It is rather like the feeling of waking up after a vivid and frightening dream, the disturbing events remaining so strongly with them that they have become disorientated and do not quite know where they are. It takes some little time to get their thoughts straightened out.

Imagine, then, how terrible it must be for a spirit being to be in this situation for many years, unable to make its presence known to loved ones still on earth, though there are the spirit helpers who come gently to explain exactly what has happened and to try to help by guiding them to the place where they should be. Sometimes the very fact that they are being told of their entry into the spirit world will be so unbelievable and abhorrent to them that all the spirit entity will want to do is to stay in familiar surroundings, becoming more and more angry about it all.

Sometimes, a spirit being who has had a particularly horrific death will be drawn back to the spot where this took place and will need much persuasion to leave it.

Evette was one such spirit personality, who came to me as I sat in that hotel lounge in Paris. Saint Saba and Grampy Danter took me on an out-of-body-experience, back in time, showing me exactly what had happened to her on that dark, wet night many years ago. She had been walking the streets, "plying her trade" as usual. Some of the money she earned would be used to buy food for the homeless street urchins who roamed the city in those days. Suddenly, a tall man dressed in top hat and tails stepped out of the shadows, grabbed her roughly, holding a hand tightly over her mouth, and flung her to the ground.

"He kept hitting me," Evette told me, "and I couldn't breathe as he squeezed my throat. The next thing I remember was looking down at my limp body lying in the gutter, but there was no pain and the man had disappeared. I went back home, but could not make anyone see me. It is so lonely now. Please show me where to go to be with other people."

So, taking her by the hand, Grampy Danter, Saint Saba and I gently guided her to a spirit hospital where Angelina, my French nun, came to take care of her.

Another time, as I sat meditating quietly in my sanctuary, the spirit form of a young merchant seaman appeared before me. His face looked so wan, pale and utterly miserable, as he told me he had perished in the last world war when his ship was torpedoed.

"My mother is still grieving for me, but no matter how much I try to attract her attention to tell her I am alive and well she doesn't see me," he said.

I saw immediately that he must be rescued. As my spirit left my body to go to him, he showed me everything that had happened on that dreadful night, and I experienced it all – desperately clawing at the water to avoid being sucked under; seeing other men struggling to keep their heads above the high pounding waves; lungs almost bursting as water flooded into them; and I went under, down, down into blackness.

After that dreadful experience we persuaded him to come with us to a spirit rehabilitation hospital where we knew he would at last find peace.

Another time during my meditation, a young man in the Air Force came and stood silently before me. He had been earthbound since the First World War.

"I was turning the propeller of a plane, but didn't get out of the way in time and had my head cut off. It was my fault of course," he said wryly. "It's awful now, because I don't know where I'm supposed to be and what to do."

His voice tailed off sounding almost in despair, so we rescued him by taking him to spirit people who would know exactly how to help.

Some of the most horrific sights I have had to see is when accident victims "show" me exactly what happened and what they had to endure at the time.

One day, friends and I were travelling by car along a narrow country lane, when I suddenly "knew" that there had been a bad accident somewhere up ahead. I turned to warn the others, but almost immediately as we rounded a sharp bend there it was – two overturned cars, and beside one in the middle of the road, the mangled body of a very young man. We were all so shocked and could hardly believe our eyes.

Fortunately, there was an inn nearby and the landlord had already telephoned the police and ambulance, who arrived on the scene in no time at all. The police quickly waved us on for there was no way we could be of help.

All the way home we sat silently, reflecting on the tragedy of that boy, losing his life in that dreadful way at such a young age. I could not get him out of my mind.

Later that evening, whilst sitting quietly listening to some soothing music and trying to free my thoughts from the day's sad events, Saint Saba suddenly appeared with Grampy Danter and said: "That young man needs your help, my child. He's still wandering about, close to the accident. We must help him."

So, on an out-of-body trip I went to the young man, who was terribly agitated and bewildered, to say: "Come with us. We will take you to people who will help you. Don't be afraid."

He took my hand and we guided him away from that dreadful place, finding a member of his family in the spirit world who greeted him warmly so we knew he was in good hands.

Here, I must hasten to say that by no means every spirit who has passed over in tragic circumstances will become earthbound. Many accept what has happened to them and will accompany the spirit helper quite peacefully, happy with their new life in such beautiful surroundings. From my own out-of-body travels, I know how very idyllic the spirit world is.

When I was working as a receptionist in Mama's hairdressing salon, a little girl whom we will call Katie often came in to have her hair cut. We knew that her home life was far from being a happy one, so when she used to "pop in for a little chat" between trims, members of the staff would give her a packet of crisps and some sweets. She seemed quite happy and content just to watch everything that went on. We all became very fond of the bright eyed, vibrant little girl.

One afternoon, her mother brought her into the salon for her usual trim. When Katie asked if she could stay for a while afterwards, one of the staff said to the mother, "If it's all right with you for her to stay with us, I'll bring her home safely later." This she did.

However, about a week later her mother came to tell us that Katie had gone missing the night before, and we were all horrified to hear that little Katie's body had been discovered by the police in a ditch, brutally murdered. Her killer was never found. We felt so dreadfully sad. How we missed that little girl's bright chatter.

Some time later, Katie's earthbound spirit form came to me. As I was rescuing her, she told me how her murder had taken place. It seemed to me, though, that she was holding back somehow, blocking out from my sight the identity of the murderer.

Now, Katie often comes back to me as a happy, well adjusted child, but every time I have asked her to tell me who the murderer is, she has become terribly upset and agitated, saying, "No, I don't want to tell you," vanishing quickly from my sight to avoid any more questions.

I feel certain that it must have been someone well-known to her, and in spite of what happened she still wished to shield them. One day, she will relent and give me a name or description which will, perhaps, save another child from a similar fate.

When we pass into spirit world, we do not sprout wings, become angels, float on clouds and play harps. What a strange notion that

is! No, the person we are on earth will remain the same in spirit –
we do not change. Sometimes, I find that it takes quite a lot of gentle
persuasion before a spirit entity can be rescued from earthly
conditions.

One evening Grampy Danter brought a Red Indian Chief to me
whose name is White Cloud. Later he became a very strong guide. At
the time he was distressed because his daughter, Moona, who many
years previously had been killed by soldiers raiding their encampment,
refused to accompany her father and mother to the "Happy Hunting
Ground" so revered by Red Indians as the place where all their
ancestors awaited them.

Moona also appeared as White Cloud spoke to me, a beautiful
brown eyed girl with raven black braids, but with such a look of
desperation on her face that it was pitiful to see.

"The soldiers came," she said. "We were all frightened, but I picked
up my papoose and hid under some skins on the floor of our teepee and
stayed there until a white man found me. I ran from him, holding the
little one tightly against me. Outside there was much noise, guns firing,
women screaming then a sharp pain in my head as a bullet hit me. All
became still, and I knew what had happened."

Red Indian children are taught from an early age about the world of
spirit.

The young girl became more and more agitated as she went on: "My
poor little papoose lay crying on the ground. I stayed close by not
knowing what to do, so angry because my life had been taken away
from him and wondering if there were any of the women left in the
camp who might care for him for me."

White Cloud then broke in, adding: "Several of us who were already
in the spirit world went to Moona to take her from that carnage, but she
would not leave the child. We all waited with her, trying to calm her.
When the soldiers went away we could see the bodies of so many of
our tribe lying everywhere. Many of our ancestors went to help their
troubled spirits. Suddenly, a squaw who had been thrown to the ground
and knocked senseless, sat up, came over to the crying child, gathered
it up tenderly in her arms and walked to her own teepee. We all
followed, but later had to leave. Moona has stayed watching over her
boy ever since."

It took many months to rescue Moona, but now she occasionally
comes back with White Cloud to show me that, at last, happiness has

come to her by caring for young children who arrive in the spirit world.

Of course, there are spirit beings who do not want to return to earthly conditions, especially if they have had a hard and painful life. My own Grandma Thomas comes back only rarely because she tells me there is such a wonderful opportunity for everyone to learn anything they wish and to gain the knowledge that it was impossible for her to do during her hard working earthly life. She finds it all so interesting and rewarding that apart from her occasional appearance when coming to visit the few remaining members of her family, she is just happy to be where she is.

It is difficult to explain this to people who have lost dear ones and been going to medium after medium in the hope of receiving some kind of communication from them, yet constantly leaving disappointed. In such cases, when they come to me for help, gentle Angelina will stand behind them, her healing hands on their head, soothing and calming. Grampy Danter will give me a message from the spirit personality concerned, which will be very reassuring.

On the other hand, in the case of suicides, I find that so many of them bitterly regret having taken their own life, especially when they realise what misery it caused members of their families left behind. Often, they beg me to find a way of telling their relatives they are sorry for what they did, but now all is well.

Sometimes, I have to deal with some very frightening and violent spirit personalities indeed. I remember a case where a man named Mike had taken his life. When he was just squeezing the trigger of the gun he realised suddenly that nothing was worth dying for and changed his mind, but it was too late! Afterwards he became tormented and aggressive, shouting at me that "It was so damned unfair," saying: "We should be given a second chance. It was all too quick. Before I knew it my life was finished and there's no going back. What hope is there for me?"

"Let me help you," I said soothingly. "We will go together to the people who can help you."

Reluctantly at first, he followed me. I took him to a place where willing spirit helpers greeted us warmly and guided him to a spirit rehabilitation hospital. I knew that he would, from then onwards, be in good hands and on returning to my body felt that a good job had been done.

After being rescued, a spirit entity can make the choice of either finding something useful to do in the spirit world or return as guides to help mediums such as myself. This has been the case with several of mine.

People often call at my home for help, feeling completely shattered after someone in their family has committed suicide. One young girl, in great distress after her father had killed himself, sobbed: "I'm so frightened for poor dad, because we all know that what he did was a sin, and he will not be allowed into the Kingdom of Heaven. What will happen to him, Sally Jane?"

Very gently, I explained that no matter what a person's colour, culture or creed, the route of the spirit to the next dimension after it leaves the body at death is the same for everyone, no matter what the circumstances.

However, I can fully understand what distress the suicide of a member of a family can cause, for twice in my life I have had this harrowing experience.

The first time, it was my Auntie Enid, about 20 years ago. I had gone to stay for a few days with my friends living in Dover. On the second night there I awoke suddenly in a cold sweat, seeing the vision of the dead body of a woman lying on the floor in an empty room. Nearby lay a shoe which I recognised instantly as being one of a pair belonging to Aunt Enid. She was a very intellectual lady, liked by everybody, who always wanted to give love and friendship to all around her. She did, however, have a serious ear condition and nerve trouble, which made it very difficult for her to express herself, often becoming irritable and impatient with people.

Next morning, I decided not to tell my friends about my vision, but during the day Mama telephoned to say that Aunt Enid had "gone missing" from home and the police were looking for her. The shock of this news, coming so soon after my psychic experience made me feel quite ill, becoming very withdrawn. My friends feared for my health and thought it would be better for me to return home.

At that time, Auntie Doris was still alive and met me at the station. Mama was unable to do so because she was looking after Grandma Thomas.

One look at Auntie Doris' serious face prepared me for the worst.

"Before we go home, Sally Jane," she said, "let us find somewhere and have a cup of tea because there's something we need to talk about." Little did she realise that I knew what she was about to say.

"The police have found Aunt Enid in an empty house. She had been dead for several days after taking a lot of tablets. You know Enid kept saying that life had become intolerable and that it would be better to end it all, but nobody believed it would happen."

It was a very emotional time for my family. A short time later I went to a small Spiritualist church in Barry where, by coincidence, a lady was talking about suicides and the "Lower regions, where they go to walk for ever in darkness." This upset me so much that back home in my sanctuary I prayed and prayed to God for Aunt Enid's soul to go in peace.

Saint Saba came and spoke gently to me: "My child, while it is never a good thing to take one's life, the spirit world knows only too well all the reasons why people do this. When it happens, though, they are never harshly judged, but helped by loving souls who have chosen to do this work. They will encourage those troubled spirit beings to take up some kind of duty which will, in turn, help them to progress along their spiritual path. However, those poor souls who remain on earth will need to be rescued by mediums who choose to do so. Very soon, my child, your help will be needed."

Some months later Aunt Enid came back to me, wearing the mauve dress which her daughter had made for her, also the hearing aid which everyone was so accustomed to seeing. She stood beside my bed, looking so forlorn, that straightaway I set about rescuing her. Without a word, Aunt Enid followed me to Higher Realms, where I left her in good hands.

Later, she came back to help as one of my guides, particularly when we have to deal with suicidal tendencies, because she wants to try and prevent other people making the same mistake as herself.

Often, when I'm giving a church demonstration, other mediums besides myself see Aunt Enid walking along the aisle pointing people out to me and saying, "Please come here, Sally Jane as this person needs your help badly."

She tells me often that she did not wander in darkness after being rescued and, in fact, that everyone in the spirit world was very kind. What a joy, too, to find that not only was her hearing perfect, but all the nervousness and tension had vanished.

"I long to tell the family of my deep sorrow for causing them so much distress and pain," she said. I promised to do this for her.

It is not acceptable to me when people say that suicide is a "coward's way out" or "They must have been very weak-minded to do such a thing." On the contrary, I'm certain that a person needs to be very strong actually to take their life. No matter what terrible trouble or pain may come to me I could never do so.

Not many years ago, Carol, a very dear friend of mine – a lovely young woman with a good husband and beautiful children and seemingly everything to live for – committed suicide. It hurt and puzzled me so much, because she had always seemed full of life and so very happy. So far, Carol has not returned. There is no way, as yet, of finding out what made her do it.

I always feel extremely sorry for parents of young people who take their own life. These youngsters are so filled with remorse and long to ask for forgiveness.

A Mr and Mrs Barratt came to my home with a photograph of their 17-year-old son, Andrew, who had killed himself. They also handed me one of his sweaters, saying, "If only our boy would come and talk to us."

Almost immediately, Andrew appeared in my sanctuary, excited at this opportunity of giving his parents a message.

"Please tell Mum and Dad that I know how stupid it was, but at the time all those difficult exams got me down and I just couldn't cope. I didn't mean to hurt them like this. Please say how very sorry I am." Andrew's parents were overjoyed.

Another time, a lovely young girl came to see me for a private sitting. As she was shown into my sanctuary, a young man entered close beside her. He told me he had been killed in a car accident shortly before he and his fiancée were to be married.

"She grieves so badly, but please say that I'll always be near all her life and will wait until it is her time to come over."

The sad young lady wept as I repeated what the man had said, and told me that I had described him in great detail. She was overcome with emotion, leaving my sanctuary in a much happier frame of mind.

There are a few instances where my psychic gifts cannot help. This makes me terribly sad.

For several nights running, during my meditation a beautiful young lady appeared to me, wearing a wedding dress and carrying a bouquet of white roses. Her sweet face looked so crestfallen as she said that on her wedding day, after the reception, she had gone up to the bedroom to change into going away clothes and suddenly felt an intense pain in the head.

"I seemed to be floating towards the ceiling. People were running about screaming, but looking down on them all it seemed just like a dream until my grandmother, who died a few years ago, came and told me I had entered the spirit world. Taking hold of my hand, she tried to persuade me to go with her, but I did not want to leave mum, dad or Peter, my new husband. Even though they obviously couldn't see me, I desperately wanted them to know of my love for them. Please can you help me."

However, no details of her family or their whereabouts were given.

Another time, a young girl, also in a wedding dress, appeared during my meditation.

"Please, please help," she implored. "I want my husband to know that I am always near, even though he cannot see me, and love him very much. He is so unhappy that my life on earth ended in a car crash on our wedding day. Can you please find him? Ali is half Iranian, has dark hair and eyes, with an olive complexion."

Sadly, with so few details, it is not possible for me to help.

There is also a little girl called Margaret, who sometimes appears besides my wheelchair as I sit doing taped sittings. She is such a pretty child, 11 years old, with lovely dark hair and eyes, but a rather sallow complexion. Dressed in a white blouse, pleated gym-slip, white socks and a red-team sash, she points to a scar on her left hand where she once cut herself.

"I was running home from school because Mummy was giving me a birthday party," explained Margaret. "I didn't look to see if any cars were coming before crossing the road and was knocked down." She always begs me, "Please can you find my mummy and daddy to tell them that I am all right?"

Apparently, this happened about 20 years ago, but Margaret will not leave earthly conditions until certain that her parents have got the message.

There is also another aspect of rescue work which I am called upon to do. Sometimes it can be quite unpleasant dealing with poltergeist activity. A poltergeist creates noise and disturbance. Frightened people come begging me to get rid of all the "evil spirits" in their home. I tell them that poltergeists are not really evil, but simply mischievous, restless souls, who are drawn to the "lower regions."

In one house I was called to, the previous owners had been

experimenting with a ouija board, and several of the rooms were haunted. Looking all around, I could plainly see several entities of somewhat weak intellect, dancing mockingly beside my wheelchair. One of them grinned at me sardonically and said, "Well, we're here, and what can *you* do about it?"

Immediately, Frankie, my protector, appeared placing himself squarely between us, which brought all their babbling to an abrupt halt. I prayed hard that the poltergeists would leave quickly. Gradually they dissolved and faded from sight.

However, the present owner of the house complained there was another ghost, which she had seen and sensed on occasions. The phantom was an old lady, who during the night kept tap, tap, tapping loudly on the floor. Alone in the haunted room, I looked around, but could see nothing unusual, when suddenly close to me there came a loud sharp crack and an elderly, grey haired lady appeared, shaking her walking stick in a very menacing manner.

"Go away!" she ordered. "I say this is my house – and I don't want anyone else in it. Go away!" Again, Frankie was there in an instant, and said: "This poor old soul needs to be rescued. Go and do your stuff!"

However, it took a great deal of explaining and persuasion from me before this was achieved, but from that time onwards it seems that everything is now quiet in the house.

Another time when giving a church demonstration, I could see three young men sitting in the front row, looking extremely ill at ease. Afterwards, they told me of being scared because frightening things were happening in the home of one of them.

"It all started after we had a go at a ouija board," one of them told me. "It was only a giggle to see if we had passed our exam. We were all at Tom's house one evening." Tom was the third boy, who just stood looking miserable and silent. "His sister came home from a jumble sale with one of those boards so we thought we'd have a go. It's his house where all the trouble is happening. His mother is now so nervous that yesterday she had to go to see the doctor, didn't she Tom?"

"Yes," he agreed. "Mum's nearly frightened out of her wits. Well, we all are," he admitted. "Someone told us you understand how to get rid of these things so we came tonight to see if you would help us."

"What kind of things have been happening?" I asked.

They replied: "Oh it's very scary because we see ghostly hands moving ornaments and things. It nearly frightened *us* to death!"

Aunt Enid appeared and explained: "Sally, my love, two of those lads have passed their exams, but that ginger-haired boy has not. Don't tell them."

I looked at the tallest boy and said: "I want you to understand that you have a psychic gift and should never play around with a ouija board without first finding out how to use it correctly and safely."

Ouija boards in themselves are neither evil nor dangerous. When used as a genuine means of communication with the spirit world, they must be treated with respect and prayer, otherwise they can attract the unwanted attention of earthbound spirits of dubious character.

The tall boy's face reddened. He looked rather like a young, embarrassed, shamefaced schoolboy. The ginger-haired youth broke in, saying: "It was all my idea. We didn't mean any harm. We only wanted to try and find out if we had passed our exams because having to wait so long for the results was getting us down. Anyway, I'm sure to have failed."

Aunt Enid said: "I'm afraid he's right. He just doesn't have an academic brain. His parents are pressing him into the wrong career. The poor boy does not want to let them down."

I said, "You find it very difficult to study and on the exam day 'freeze'." He looked at me as if I had discovered a very closely kept secret.

"Yes, that's right. I'm hopeless, but it's impossible to tell my parents that my only ambition is to be a farmer, not a lawyer like dad. They have such high hopes for me."

"Don't worry about it," I told him. "We'll ask for spiritual help, but you will have to co-operate. For the next few nights be in your bedroom, preferably between 10.30 and 11.00 when my absent healing is done. Lie quietly relaxed and pray. I will do my part. You will be surprised how God will help you and, of course, I'll come to your house." This I did the following day. It proved to be quite a battle dealing with that wayward spirit, but with the help of my guardian angels we managed in the end. Thankfully, all is now quiet.

Several weeks later he saw me again and beaming said: "You *knew* that they failed me in my exams, didn't you! Never mind. I did as you said. Waking up early one morning I was absolutely determined to make a clean breast of the whole thing to my parents. Instead of 'going up the wall,' they were very understanding about it. Dad wanted to know what career would suit me. He is coming with me for an interview at the agricultural college. It's great!"

It is wonderful what prayer and spiritual help will do.

## Chapter Eighteen

## THE NUMEROUS WAYS OF SPIRIT HELP

ALL the time I was on my working holiday in Belgium and France, Mama had been holding the fort for me at home, answering the telephone, arranging private sittings and explaining why there would be a short delay before my work could continue as usual.

On returning home, there was a huge pile of letters from many parts of the world awaiting my attention. Normally, I try to send off taped readings as soon as possible, realising that sometimes they can be a real life-line to some people, so for the next few weeks I set about dealing with them in strict rotation – and the telephone kept ringing!

It is an asset in this work to have a sense of humour, for there are sometimes some very unusual requests, mostly because some people are totally ignorant of the true nature of a medium's function.

One gentleman telephoned in a very depressed state of mind as he had become very worried about himself and was completely disenchanted with what little help various mediums were able to give him.

"Will you please answer a few questions on the phone?" he said, and proceeded to reel off from a written list about a dozen in quick succession.

"Just a minute, please," I had to break in. "Exactly how many questions are there?"

Sheepishly, he replied, "Well, er, actually, 53!"

Now, from the telephone contact with that gentleman, it was obvious to me that he had quite a strong psychic capability, but not understanding it was quite unable to cope, to the point of wondering if he was going mad! I suggested a private sitting. As we sat in my sanctuary discussing his problems, to his delight, my spirit guide brought several of his relations from the spirit world. He begged me to teach him how to develop his gift so he became another one of my students, receiving tuition by tape.

This part of my work had started to grow rapidly. Once again Saint Saba had been proved right when, long ago, he told me that I was born to teach spiritual development. It was then that a future plan formulated in my mind.

Months went busily by and I found that there were many more youngsters begging constantly for help. One young girl, Jane, telephoned, but would not tell me what was troubling her. Later in my sanctuary, it became clear that she had become frightened, but couldn't possibly tell her parents that "she kept seeing ghosts," so had come to me for help.

We talked for a long time. As I explained everything, gradually all the tension and agitation left her. This girl had mediumistic capabilities which needed to be properly developed. Her parents would have to be told – a ticklish situation – because it is never my policy to interfere in such things, but help this girl, I must!

Grampy Danter and Saint Saba advised me to contact the parents, promising me they would be very relieved when it was explained to them what was wrong with their daughter – and it happened exactly that way. Now Jane has become a very hard-working student indeed.

Occasionally, people telephone for an appointment to have their fortune told. This always makes Mama so angry. She tells them curtly, "My daughter is a medium, *not* a fortune teller!"

It never fails to amaze, and often amuse me, to hear some of the weird, wonderful and archaic ideas some people have, even in these so-called enlightened times, about mediums and their work. There is a great difference between mediums and fortune tellers.

A medium is able, through her special God-given gifts and sensitivity, to link into the spirit world and can see, hear and talk to spirit guides who bring other spirit beings. These always appear to him or her looking no different from anyone of flesh and blood. Our function is to prove beyond doubt that life goes on in another dimension, and communication with those who have passed over *is* really possible. This can be of inestimable value to people who have lost a loved one, are left grieving, desperately lonely and longing for the comfort that proof of another life can bring them. When they receive through the medium a message from their loved ones it brings them great joy to know that they are *not* lost for ever.

Readings from a pack of cards, tea leaves and the like are totally different. I have taken part in experiments set to prove the veracity of this. Several people were each given a card reading on three successive days – and each time the reading was different! Just think how many people day in, day out, handle the cards of a fortune teller, so imagine what mix of influences there must remain on them.

There is no doubt at all, though, that there are some really excellent card readers, who are able to do this so well because they possess a psychic gift. Indeed, I had a friend who was known for her tea-leaf readings, but it was quite obvious to me that she had a strong psychic capability.

"Why do you trouble to go through all that rigmarole with tea cups when you really have no need?" I asked her.

"I know it's not necessary, Sally Jane, but the type of person who comes to me to have their fortune told expects me to study the cup. It gives them confidence that what I am seeing in their cup is a real view of their future."

Each to his own, though. But no, mediums do *not* tell fortunes. Rather, they are asking for the help of their guides, and are able to show people the way through their problems and worrying situations. This is not done for any idle whim on the part of the sitter, but because of a genuine desire to use their spiritual gifts to help humanity, and are of a different standard entirely.

In a household where there is no understanding whatsoever of mediums and their work, even young children can get entirely the wrong idea.

A young mother, Mrs Evans, came to ask my help, because her small son, Tommy, had lately become "a little demon."

"It's ever since he started at a new school," she wept. "He used to be so quiet and loving, but even his teachers are complaining about him. I just don't know what's come over him."

Grampy Danter whispered to me: "The lad is finding it difficult to keep up with the other boys in the higher grade and it is a great strain on him. He needs healing."

I saw Angelina standing behind Mrs Evans, putting soothing hands on the head of the distraught lady. I promised to give Tommy absent healing, which proved to be a great success.

Some weeks later she called again at my home bringing Emma, her small daughter. Whilst Mama and Mrs Evans were chatting in the hall, the little girl came into my sanctuary and stood beside my wheelchair with a puzzled expression on her face. Children think very deeply about things. Apparently, she had seen that there was no car in the drive. Dada was in it at the time.

"How do you go out to the shops for your groceries, Auntie Sally? Do you fly there like a fairy because I know that you do magic things?"

It was very hard for me to suppress my laughter, but I asked, "What makes you think that, sweetheart?"

She replied, "Well, mummy tells everybody that what you have done for Tommy has worked like magic." I adore children and their innocent, spontaneous remarks!

Another unusual request was when a Mr and Mrs Jones called to ask if my spirit guides would help them by seeing their son and daughter who had been discovered experimenting with drugs.

"We just couldn't believe that Jenny and Jason would ever do such a thing," Mrs Jones sobbed. "We are at the end of our tether wondering how to handle it. Our children have changed so much. Their behaviour is upsetting our whole family life – cheeky, bad language and dirty habits. It is nearly impossible to recognise them as the same children. Please, is there anything that you can do?"

I made an appointment to see the two teenagers the next day. They duly arrived, bringing with them two friends, another boy and girl. They all looked extremely unkempt, wearing dirty clothing with hair that looked as if it had not been washed for months.

Mama showed them into my sanctuary, purposely leaving the door ajar. The sudden sight of me sitting alone in my wheelchair was quite unexpected to them. Straight away they tried to intimidate me. They swaggered around the room, picking things up and putting them down again in a different place, whispering rude remarks just loud enough so that I could hear.

Sitting silently for a few minutes without saying a word, Grampy Danter and Frankie, my protector, appeared before me.

I said: "Well, you've all come here for help – and help is what you are going to get! Your behaviour is not at all funny, you know. Do you really enjoy upsetting your parents by it?"

One boy retorted rudely, "Who cares?"

Grampy Danter told me: "That one is the ring-leader and is a bad influence on the others. Tell him you know exactly what he has been doing late at nights."

I did so . . . and from his reddened, frightened face it convinced me that he most certainly had been up to no good! "Who told you?" he stormed.

Ignoring him, I spoke to Jenny, saying, "Why are you wasting your time getting into trouble when you could be doing something worthwhile, like attending art school which is your ambition?"

Jenny looked hard at me. "Yes, it is, but what's the point when there's probably no job vacant at the end of it all?"

All four began talking together, pouring out their grievances against the world, and their parents in particular. I asked them to sit down quietly and listened to each one's troubles in turn. With the help of Grampy Danter and Saint Saba they were shown the way to change various things in their lives.

After all of them had left the house, Mama came to me and said: "I didn't like leaving you alone in there, Sally Jane. The four of them looked so rough, anything could have happened to you."

I hadn't been afraid. In fact, there have only been a few times in my life when I have really experienced fear. The knowledge that my guardian angels are always around gives me complete confidence.

Years ago, though, when staying with Auntie Doris, we had planned to go for a long walk. The others went to get ready, leaving me in a downstairs room in front of a large open window which overlooked the front garden. Some youths came along, obviously bent on causing trouble and stood pulling faces and shouting abusive remarks at me.

I watched in horror as one of them opened the gate and came into the garden. He picked up a large stone from the rockery and hurled it in my direction, but thankfully it missed and I screamed. Instantly, Frankie appeared and stood in front of my wheelchair. The youth was bending over, grabbing another stone and straightened up ready to throw it when he stopped short and stood absolutely still with a look of disbelief on his face.

Shouting something to his pals, all three went running up the road as fast as they could. Hearing my scream, Mama and Auntie Doris came rushing into the room to find me shaking with fear, pointing frantically towards the window. When they looked out they could see the hooligans way up the road, still running for dear life.

Another time, a friend of mine called Alice visited our house to ask if I'd like to go for a walk with her.

"We've seen so little of each other lately, Sally Jane," she said. "It would give us the opportunity to have a long chat."

It was a quiet, sunny Sunday morning. The roads were deserted. All of a sudden, I experienced an awful feeling of evil surging over me and felt that someone was watching us as she pushed me along. Alice must have had a similar feeling as she looked over her shoulder and saw a shabbily dressed man, behaving suspiciously.

"I don't like the look of him," she said anxiously and quickened her steps, but still keeping a watchful eye on the man lurking behind us. As we drew near to some houses which had long gardens the man went through a gate and vanished from our sight. Alice blew out her breath in relief, remarking: "Well, thank goodness for that! I didn't like the look of him at all! "

Both of us felt rather foolish. Although he looked suspicious, he could have been perfectly harmless.

We continued our walk until we arrived at a small store. "I'll just pop in there and get us some sweets," Alice said, and after parking my wheelchair safely, went into the shop leaving me sitting in the warm sunshine, contented and relaxed – but not for long! Without any warning, a strong hand grasped my shoulder roughly. The man was back! Surprised and alarmed, I saw the rough fellow draw out of his badly soiled trouser pocket a crumpled bag of sweets. He held them out to me saying in a deep coarse voice, "Have one of these and we'll go for a walk, my dear." I froze as he fumbled with the wheelchair brake.

Frankie appeared in full battledress, complete with rifle and fixed bayonet, facing the man in a very threatening manner. Now, whatever it was the man saw or felt, I do not know, but with an exclamation of shocked surprise he took off down the road at great speed.

Just then, Alice came out of the shop to find me shaking like a leaf and very distressed.

"What on earth is the matter, Sally Jane?" she said, putting her arm around me, patting my shoulder comfortingly.

When I managed to tell her what had happened she exclaimed, "Now don't worry, we'll be home soon," and proceeded to push my wheelchair along faster than it had ever been pushed before! Of course, Alice was unaware that Frankie was walking with us.

Later that evening as we sat watching the news on TV, there was an urgent police report concerning a dangerous rapist who had escaped from a prison and was still at large in our area. People were warned to stay in their homes until he could he caught.

People often say to me, "It must be wonderful to know that your guardian angels can help and protect you, but how can a spirit with no earthly body do this?"

When I asked Frankie the question, he grinned broadly at me, winking his eye as if to say, "Honey, that's my secret." However, knowing what I do of spirit power, most likely Frankie is able to project some kind of restraining energy which can actually be seen or felt by anyone intending to harm me. Whatever it is, it works!

Many, many times in my life, guardian angels have alerted me to impending danger which could possibly cause me injury or harm. For example, when in Belgium, Grampy Danter told me not to take another ride on the Big Dipper because it was about to break down. Also, my life most certainly would have been lost in the car accident in which my friend was killed had not Grampy Danter filled me with a positive inner warning not to accept the invitation for an evening out.

On many occasions when in hospital, all my guardian angels have brought me great comfort by their constant reassuring presence. Once or twice before an operation, one of them explained to me exactly how it would be carried out successfully, and I felt no fear as they were pushing me on the trolley to the operating theatre.

In my work, without the help of the guides it would be impossible for me to function. Over the years, a number of spirit helpers have joined me, each ready to step forward to assist me in their own particular way when a troubled person comes for help. Some of these lovely guides have already been mentioned, but others have since joined me.

I remember about eight years ago, a lovely lady called Harriet was brought to me for healing by her son. She had suffered a complete nervous breakdown after her husband left home and just could not accept that the marriage was over. The other sons had married and moved away from the district leaving the youngest lad to cope and look after his mother by himself. During a previous telephone conversation he told that his mother had spent some time in a psychiatric hospital. Now she had come back home again, Harriet had stopped eating completely and slept very little. He was desperate to know how to handle the situation.

The medical profession is wonderful and I have a great respect for their work, but unfortunately they have no prescriptions for healing grief!

That afternoon in my sanctuary, the distraught lady, crying

uncontrollably, sat rocking backwards and forwards. It was the first time I had been called upon to deal with such a case. However, Aunt Enid came and stood behind my wheelchair with Grampy Danter, Angelina and Saint Saba, who brought with him a Mother Superior, wearing a white robe from which hung a long chain with an unusual looking crucifix.

"My child," said Saint Saba. "This is Sister Dominique who would like to join us to help with difficult cases like this."

Sister Dominique said to me: "Take both the lady's hands and hold them firmly, even though she will try very hard to pull away. We must rid her quickly of the disharmony within."

Angelina went and stood behind Harriet, placing gentle hands on her head to begin the healing. Soothing words were put into my mind by my loving guides. As I spoke them I could see a change gradually taking place. Tension lessened, tears ceased and eventually a very much calmer lady left my sanctuary.

For two or three months Harriet was brought to me for treatment until it was obvious to us all that she had been cured. "It's absolutely wonderful," her son said. "Mum's a new woman!"

A year later they both moved away from the district to start anew.

Not long afterwards when Mama and I sat quietly discussing my work, Sister Dominique came saying that she would like to tell us about her life when on earth.

"My childhood days were very happy," she said. "When later I met a wonderful young man, we both fell very much in love and planned to marry, but tragically he was killed in the war. Without him, life had no meaning. Such was my great unhappiness that all I wanted to do was shut myself away from everything but my memories.

"I joined a silent order of nuns, but found it very difficult at first to adjust to the austere surroundings of the convent, which was bitterly cold in winter. In time, I grew to love the peace and spiritual atmosphere of the place. Life once again became bearable for me, even happy, and I took on the duty of instructing novice nuns in the nursing craft."

Sister Dominique became Mother Superior, living until 80 years old, but always comes back as a young woman in the prime of life. She often says, "When I came over, how wonderful it was to find my dearest Frank waiting for me looking as young and handsome as ever, so now I always appear as he knew me before."

Sister Dominique is a wonderful healing and teaching guide and is always there when I am working on taped readings.

About seven years ago, another well-thought-of gentleman, whom I knew when he was on earth, joined my band of helpers. His name was Arnall Bloxham. Not only was he a well respected hypnotherapist, but also a most psychic and spiritual man.

We had met quite by chance. A friend of mine who knew Arnall well told him about my work. Being so interested in the subject he invited us to his home for a long talk. I found him to be a man of great wisdom with a wonderful zest for life. However, it was clear to me from the grey and murky colours in his aura that he would soon pass. It was clear he realised it as well.

Several times we visited Mr Bloxham's home and thoroughly enjoyed hearing about his work, being particularly interested to learn that hypnotic regression can be invaluable as part of treatment.

We were very sad indeed to hear soon afterwards that he had passed, but how very pleased I was when he returned to have the help of such a kind, wise, loving man.

So you see, when people come to me it is not only my help they receive, but that of many guides, who know exactly how to deal with their particular problems.

## Chapter Nineteen

## ABOUT MY MEDIUMSHIP

FOR the next few years my life and work continued busily and with many, many psychic experiences.

From time to time when the pain in my back became too unbearable, it meant that a further course of physiotherapy at the hospital was necessary. After one of these sessions I had an experience – not psychic – the awful memory of which has never left me.

When each treatment was over I enjoyed going to the children's ward and having a cheery word with each child in turn. In the beds on one side of the ward were little ones who were suffering greatly as a result of being abused badly by one or other of their parents. My heart went out to those poor little children, lying battered, bruised and silent. The sister told me that those beds were always filled with similar, sad cases.

One particular little girl called Chrissie had been so badly beaten about the head and body by her father that she was now in a coma, like a vegetable. Nobody came to visit her. Neither the staff nurse nor I knew that the father was serving a four-year prison sentence for the ill-treatment of his daughter.

That afternoon, sitting beside Chrissie, and gazing with sadness into her pale face with dark shadows under the closed eyes, I took the thin hand in mine and stroked it gently, trying so hard to convey to her somehow that there was *someone* in the world who cared during her last hours on earth. For it was clear to me from the dark greying of her aura that the suffering of the poor little lamb would soon be over.

The ward was quiet except for the occasional muffled sound of a cough, or a little groan coming from children in the nearby beds. Suddenly, I heard loud footsteps coming in my direction and a heavily built, very unkempt man approached the bed, holding in his hand a steaming cup of coffee which he had obviously just got from the dispensing machine.

Without warning – and to my absolute horror – he flung the hot liquid over Chrissie's face. I screamed, the man turned quickly away and started to run, but fortunately a doctor had just entered the ward in time to see what had taken place. He pushed the man to the floor overpowering him, shouting, "Quickly! Get the police."

I sat slumped in my wheelchair, trembling from shock, as nurses ran back and forth trying to calm the children who had seen it all. Sister bent over Chrissie, treating her blistering face. Soon, two policemen appeared, handcuffed the struggling man and took him away. By now my tears were flowing freely. One of the nurses, also with tears in her eyes, came to me and said: "Come on, love, I'll take you out to the ambulance. The driver will soon get you home."

The next day, the young doctor told me that the man had only just been released from prison and went straight to the hospital to seek revenge on his daughter, blaming her for his four years in prison.

It took me many weeks really to get over it. One night I asked Saint Saba, "Why did that dreadful man do such a terrible thing to a poor little defenceless girl?"

He replied; "My child, if you looked deeply within him, you would see that he was brutally abused as a child, so now feels he must get his revenge. He has a very troubled soul."

Mercifully, soon after Chrissie passed away, and I was so thankful to know that at last she was free of her painful life.

Lying in bed at night my mind going over it all, I remembered another child, Mary, who was in hospital with me years ago, when we were both five years old. She was a brittle bone child and had been in hospital almost since birth, not abused, but apparently abandoned by her young mother, her father being unknown. One morning the mother, after being contacted and summoned by the matron, arrived to make arrangements for Mary to board at the same special school which I was about to enter.

When her mother had gone, Mary said to me, "Who was that lady, Sally Jane?"

"That was your Mama," I replied.

She looked at me in disbelief and said: "Oh no, it wasn't. I haven't got one."

Later when the doctor explained to her that she would be leaving the hospital to go to school, Mary just looked at him with wide, troubled eyes, but said nothing.

That night, when all the children were asleep, I saw her get out of bed clutching her doll in her arms and deliberately crash her leg hard against the wall, knowing full well that this would break her bones. I called out for the nurse, as Mary fell to the floor in great pain. You see, she was so frightened of leaving the hospital, which was the only home that she had ever known, she carried out this plan to ensure her staying there.

Although I was able to do my psychic work as usual during my "free time" when taking a short rest, Chrissie kept coming into my mind. On the following Sunday afternoon, seeing my restlessness, Mama said, "It's such a nice day, my lovely, why don't we go out into the garden and I'll do some weeding?"

As I sat in my wheelchair under the branches of a shady tree watching Mama's bent back as she worked busily on the borders, to my great joy Auntie Doris appeared, standing close beside her. Mama, of course, sensed something and looked up into the smiling face of her much-loved sister. With an exclamation of surprise and delight, she stood up and put out her arms. I heard Auntie Doris say, "Liz, let's walk the way we used to do."

Linking arms, they walked slowly towards me, smiling happily, until Auntie Doris gradually faded from sight. Her unexpected appearance lifted me completely out of my depression, which I'm sure was Auntie Doris' intention.

It is often said to me, "Sally Jane, working as you do all day with so much sickness and despair, don't you ever become despondent?"

My answer is always the same: "Never! To me it is great privilege to possess the gifts which make me a 'seer for God,' which is what I prefer to call myself."

People should realise by now there are those of us in the world like myself – and always have been, even before records were kept – who are born with special psychic gifts which enable us to see, hear and converse with spirit beings for the purpose of helping and bringing comfort to humanity.

My life is not all gloom and despondency. Seeing what happiness my gifts bring fills me with great joy and satisfaction. Being a healer and medium is my chosen profession, although we who are doing this work must beware of going over the top or, as the Americans say, "become a screw-ball." By living a normal life we keep a balanced outlook. There should be no stigma attached to being a medium.

In more recent years, I have found that when people come to me for a private sitting, they are so amazed when I have reunited them with their loved ones that afterwards they want to sit and ask more questions about my work, especially the young ones.

A medium is a channel for the spirit realms, rather like a bridge between this world and the next. Every medium works on a different frequency. My spiritual development has taken place over a number of years until it has reached such a highly sensitive level that, as I have been told by other mediums, if it were any higher I would be in the next world!

I think that today's society is in great need of compassion, help and understanding and we, as healers and mediums, have to prove that no matter who people are, or where they come from, we are workers for God and have a great responsibility to do this to the very best of our ability.

Saint Saba always taught me the great importance of fasting before doing any psychic work, because this bodily emptiness makes it much easier for Spirit to work through me. All I allow myself during my working hours is fluids, but I eat normal meals when my work is done for the day.

Many times in hospital, before an operation, other patients would be grumbling to the nurses because they had been given no breakfast and couldn't understand why going without food didn't worry me a bit!

Before seeing anyone for a private sitting in my sanctuary, I spend some time in meditation and pray for God's guidance. This is most important. When the person is shown into my room I ask them to sit down in front of me, take both their hands and study their aura, the colours of which tells me many things. Here is what the various hues depict.

Orange      – Stands for strength of character.
Silver      – For a highly developed attunement with other people, a caring person.
Cherry      – Persons will stand up for others as well as themselves.
Turquoise   – A person is sometimes too trusting of others.
Pale Green  – Healing is taking place.
Dark Red    – Person is unable to stand firmly against adversity.
Pink        – Loving person. Saint Saba always appears outlined with

a lovely bold pink.

Brown      – Shows that knowledge will be earned by hard work.

Blue        – Person inclined to mild depression or a "fit of the blues."

Grey       – Illness.

The next step is to allow my mind to be raised to a higher vibration, to the level and identity of all my guides who have come to help. For me, the pathway to the spirit world is easy, just like tuning in to a TV channel or dialling a telephone number and working through all the different wires to reach the wavelength required. It is all a question of attuning the mind, through meditation and prayer. In this way, after many years, we are able to reach the highest spiritual frequencies. As for my own feelings when reaching the highest vibrations, all my pains disappear, leaving me completely unaware of any discomfort, even when recovering from operations.

A simple explanation of what happens next is that it is rather like having a switch in my brain which, when turned on, will illuminate every part of the sitter, right into their very heart and thoughts. I then experience all their pains, both physical and mental, and can see beneath it all, for as mentioned before, within our subconscious is registered our every thought and emotion throughout our lifetime. All these have a profound effect upon our body, even causing illness.

When I am sufficiently attuned, a spirit visitor will appear, perhaps a husband, father, mother, son or daughter, or anyone with a link of love with the sitter. My guides will then tell me many things to pass on to the person who has come for help, so as to give proof of their identity.

Each guide will communicate with me in their own particular way. Sometimes they do not speak, but will show symbols, which Saint Saba taught me to interpret right at the start of my development. Here are a few examples of symbols and their meanings:

| SYMBOL | INTERPRETATION |
| --- | --- |
| Red tape | – Legal matters to be resolved. |
| Water lily | – Disappointment with a need to overcome it. |
| Clear water | – A clear pathway to go forward. |
| Cloudy water | – Things need to be cleared up. |
| Marionette | – Person is being pulled in many directions. |
| Wire rolled up | – A problem must be cut through. |

| | |
|---|---|
| Clown | – A sad bereavement, but the sitter will put on a clown's face for the benefit of the family. |
| Mountain | – A struggle within. |
| Weeping willow | – Before things come right, there must be many tears. |
| Canoe being paddled | – Person's life going in the right direction. |
| Gloves | – Things must be handled gently with kid gloves. |
| New baby | – Going into a new life pattern which must be handled delicately. |
| Deeds | – Some documents to be signed. |
| Ladders | – Must struggle to climb high. |
| Moccasins | – A new beginning. |
| Books piled high | – Must seek further knowledge for a certain situation. |
| Desert | – This is how a person's life may seem to them at present, but remember that Bedoins live there so it is possible to survive such conditions. |
| Monk with bowed head | – Religious matter to be sorted out. |
| Monk with head held high | – Will find answer to problem very quickly. |
| Boxing gloves held down | – Person will need to fight their way out of a situation. |
| Boxer throwing in the towel | – Must struggle or the fight will be lost. |
| Bee | – Person always on the go. |
| Cracked object | – Delicate matter to handle. |
| Maze | – Difficulty in finding a way through a family problem, but things will turn out as planned. |
| Bright star | – The person is like a jewel and will shine in their life. The scales of life will always balance. |
| Olive branch | – Peace will come in a certain situation. |
| Weight | – Person feels weighted down by responsibility. |

| | |
|---|---|
| Uprooted tree | – A new dwelling. |
| Raging waters | – Family needs calming. |
| Red Carpet | – Special occasion soon. |
| Hammer | – Person must rebuild life. |
| Butterfly | – Delicate situation to come. |
| Lion | – Shows great strength of character. |

These are but a few examples of the way that some of my guides convey things to me, though most of the time I hear their voices clearly giving me information which will benefit the sitter.

Very occasionally, I come into contact with sceptics, who use abusive words and destructive remarks to me, denouncing mediums as people working against God. They could not be more wrong!

I am not out to convert anybody since each of us has a completely free choice of thought and actions, but when this sort of person begins airing their totally misguided views, having obviously never gone deeply into the subject to try and understand what it is all about, it irritates me a lot. I will go out of my way to prove to them the true value and purpose of my God-given gifts.

There was a really hard-bitten sceptic such as this who sat in the front of the church when I was giving a demonstration. This man had been brought along, much against his will, and was sitting next to his wife, most uncomfortably on his seat as if longing to escape from the place.

Aunt Enid appeared close by and told me that his wife had been told about my work. Because she was so unhappy and upset at losing her mother, whom she had nursed for years, the woman hoped that she would receive some reassurance that the old lady was all right.

Almost immediately, the elderly mother came through and stood beside her troubled daughter, telling me numerous personal things to convey to her, which I did. Several other relations came. When I described them in every detail the lady was overjoyed.

Then I turned to the husband. Grampy Danter, Saint Saba, Nana Watts and Aunt Enid gathered all around giving me a complete picture of the man's life, past and present, with many personal details. On hearing it all, he was completely flabbergasted.

The fact that his mother had been able to prove so conclusively her identity brought such a change over him. He looked at me in shocked amazement, his face turning from red to white. I could see that she had proved, beyond doubt, her existence. He began asking questions, receiving answers which amazed him. Tears filled his eyes.

Afterwards I said, "Now Sir, can you still honestly feel that my work is against God when it is He who has given me the gift to bring comfort and knowledge to people?"

Still somewhat overcome by his experience he mumbled: "My dear, my dear, I didn't realise what it was all about. We will now find out much more about the whole subject."

When hearing people on TV chat shows airing their views about mediums it makes me very sad to hear them say it is wrong for anyone to "hold on to their dead" by going to one. Obviously they have never investigated the subject or been devastated by the death of a loved one.

One of the purposes of this book is to explain fully about psychic matters, exactly what mediumship is, and why these gifts are bestowed on us like precious jewels to be used to ease people's grief. For with the loving compassion and guidance from Spirit they will be able to pick up the pieces of their life – and once again go forward.

It is not always because someone has lost a family loved one that people come to me.

A tearful young lady telephoned one evening saying rather hesitatingly: "I hope you don't mind my ringing, and most probably you will think me foolish, but last week my beautiful horse died and my friends keep telling me that animals have no souls. They simply decay in the ground if they are buried."

I assured her hastily, saying, "Well, my lovely, your friends are wrong," rather angered by the person who had told her such a thing. "Of course your lovely horse has a soul. All animals have. His will go to a place where he will be completely happy with lush fields, crystal clear water and sunshine, in the company of many others like himself, all living happily together. At times he may return to the field where he was so contented with you here on earth. If you stand very still, no doubt you will be strongly aware of his presence."

I could thoroughly understand that young lady's grief, for several times in my life the sad experience of losing a much-loved animal has befallen me. As anyone who has ever kept a pet will know, the love and loyalty we receive from them is sometimes far greater than that given to us by human beings. We become so attached to them they really are part of our family.

In my teens, I had a beautiful mare called Tess, who was kept in a field on my friend's farm. One day, though, Tess became ill, and the vet broke the news to me that she would have to be put down. With a heavy heart I told him, "I know there is nothing else that can be done for her, but I want to be there when it happens."

He put his arm around my shoulder and said gently, "Are you sure you want to watch it?"

Miserably, I nodded my head as the vet did what he had to do. Slowly, as I watched, Jess' spirit arose out of her body and was set free.

Often I have been nudged awake by the spirit of my friend's lovely Golden Retriever, Kimmy. Pat was a dear friend of mine who sadly took her own life. She and Kimmy were inseparable. Pat stands smiling at me, looking exactly as she did in life with her dark brown hair and eyes, showing me they are happily reunited.

Years ago my own little Poodle, Tina, became ill during one of my visits to Auntie Doris. Together we took her to the veterinary surgeon, who had to put her down. We were so shattered by it that neither of us could eat or sleep properly for several days. Back home again, several weeks later, Mama went out into the garden to relax on a sunbed. As she lay there, out of the corner of her eye she saw a movement in the grass under the apple tree. And there was Tina, panting slightly with out-stretched paws in her customary manner. Mama sat up and called, "Tina, Tina, good girl, come here."

Tina wagged her tail, but gradually disappeared. I have often seen Tina sitting beside my wheelchair, showing me that she is still around.

There are many ways in which I am able to "analyse" a person. Earlier on I mentioned psychometry, which is a medium's psychic sensing by holding an article in the hand and being able to feel the vibrations of the owner. These can be such things as an ear-ring, a watch-strap, pen, brooch or a photograph, etc. If someone sends me a photograph of themselves with another person to psychometrise it is more difficult because I pick up the vibration of both of them. Even when covering up the other person's picture a small amount of vibration still comes from them, so usually I work only on the letter.

An amazing assortment of such things are sent to me to be analysed – a piece of string, an empty notebook, feathers, playing cards, etc. Each one tells me many things.

When psychometrising I place my hands over the article and Diane, my little guide, who during her life was multi-handicapped and blind, comes to me and puts her small hands over mine. Immediately I feel all the vibrations of the owner of the article, their moods, temperament and character. One of my other guides who has come to help will bring a relative from the other world to communicate and give messages which will be of such comfort to someone they have left behind.

The same thing applies when psychometrising a garment or object which belonged to someone now in the spirit world. As soon as I hold it for a minute or two, I am able to pick up the illness which caused the death of the person and get a clear picture of the life they led.

When people are unable to come for a private sitting they write asking for a taped reading, sending a photograph.

One lady telephoned me in great distress after the sudden death of her husband. She was devastated, feeling so lonely and let down because of the lack of help the vicar of her local church, which she attended regularly, had given her. In desperation – and on the recommendation of a friend – she telephoned me.

As we were speaking, the spirit form of her husband came through the door of my sanctuary and sat down in an armchair. I described him to her in every detail. He had white hair and blue eyes, and wore a white shirt and light coloured trousers. The husband told me several things to say which proved his identity conclusively and so amazed his wife that she was laughing and crying at the same time on the other end of the phone. She begged me to book an appointment for a private sitting, which I did gladly.

When she came to the house, sitting in front of me in my sanctuary I was able to reunite husband and wife again together with several members of their family. The result was that her outlook on life completely changed. She now knew that her husband *was* alive and well so there was no need to pine away in wretchedness.

Occasionally, when there are many, many problems to overcome, it is just not possible to do so all on one taped reading or private sitting. Remember, I am dealing with people's emotions. It is my responsibility gradually and gently to work through all the hidden layers of their problems, one at a time, rather like peeling an onion. I honestly believe that after giving a reading it is not the end of the matter and always tell people that if they feel the need to talk to me concerning what has been given them I am only a phone-call away, ready and willing to help them further.

It is not my usual practice to telephone people unasked, but sometimes something happens which makes me change my rule.

One morning Mama came into the sanctuary bringing the mail. In a letter from a lady requesting a taped reading for her daughter, Emma, was a photograph of a lovely young girl sitting in a wheelchair. From the limp, twisted little body, I knew it was a muscular condition affecting the spine. Holding the picture in my hand I said to Mama, "This little girl is in Spirit, but her mother has asked for a taped reading, as if she were still alive."

As I spoke there came a pleading little voice saying, "Please, please ring my mummy."

Emma appeared, dressed in a white top with a blue motif on the pocket, grey trousers, orange leg-warmers and dark socks. How could I refuse her request?

Her mother was so surprised and pleased when I telephoned, though there was such loneliness and sadness in her voice, which told me how difficult she found it to accept her daughter's death. How overjoyed she was on being told that it was Emma who had asked me to ring. We spoke for some time. Suddenly Emma appeared to me again, her face wreathed in smiles, saying, "Please tell Mum that I don't have to be in a wheelchair now and Grandma is here with me."

The grandmother came and stood with her arm around Emma. Tears and exclamations of delight came from her mother as I explained it to her. She thanked me again and again, at the same time booking a private sitting.

When children pass over, they are taken immediately to the Higher Realms to be looked after by relations or caring spirit people who love youngsters. Even so, whenever I hear of a child's passing it always saddens me to know how much grief is felt by the parents.

Flower reading is another form of psychometry. If someone picks a flower and holds it between their hands for a short while it can be analysed in exactly the same way as an article or photograph.

Every morning of my life, before my psychic work begins, I spend some time in meditation and prayer with Saint Saba. Prayer to me is most important. As the work on each tape begins, an individual prayer is said for every person and their loved-ones come close as I proceed with it. My guides gather around to help me.

Prayer opens one's psychic channels which enables me when holding the photograph to put myself in their position. This is the sort of prayer I use:

"O Father, grant that I may be an instrument of peace, love and tranquillity in all that I do, in all that I see, and be able to give glimpses of truth.

"Dear Father, you have granted me gifts to be a vessel for your love, and I will serve you humbly daily, as I go through life helping those who are distressed and weary, knowing that you are with us all. Amen."

Many people write to me after receiving their tape, saying how much they liked my starting it with a prayer. Prayers are of great importance in my life. I will always remember an incident in hospital which caused me great unhappiness.

I made friends with a young girl called Marion. We were both going to have an operation the same afternoon. A deaconess came into the ward and prayed for children whose parents were Church of England, but did not come to Marion or myself. Upset and tearful because of this, my friend said, "Sally Jane, will you pray for us please?"

This is the prayer I said: "O, Lord Jesus, grant that Marion and I will come through our adversity and pain. We are friends now and will be forever. We are a little afraid of what is to come and need your blessing. We place ourselves into your keeping and ask very humbly that we will live and be able to see our parents and friends again. Amen."

People may say, "Why is prayer so important to you?" I reply, "Being a Christian and a server for God, I know that only prayer can see us through our earthly life, can open doors, can open up our life. Some may be wealthy, healthy and successful, never giving a thought to prayer, but when something devastating happens in their life and they are 'walking in the wilderness' then they will cry out for help to God. He never fails us."

Mama and Grandma Thomas taught me about prayer at a very early age and we always prayed together. I remember the first time I prayed to God on my own. At five years old and being very unhappy at my first school, never having been away from home before and feeling very homesick, it was made worse by the fact that the school rule insisted children were not allowed to have any visitors whatsoever for one month after being admitted – and I had only been there two weeks.

Someone had taken me out into the grounds and left me alone in my wheelchair beside a large pool where there was a fountain playing. Feeling utterly miserable, I decided to tell God all about it and closed my eyes and prayed.

"O, Jesus, may I please be back with my family? Bless them, guard and protect them and please find a way so that I can see Mama again soon. Amen."

On opening my eyes to my amazement I saw a pretty little spirit girl in a lovely dark blue dress with a lace collar, standing on the other side of the fountain. She smiled and called to me, "Don't cry, you will be seeing your mummy tomorrow."

Grampy Danter also appeared and said: "Yes, my angel, the little one has come to tell you this. You must believe her."

They both faded from sight, leaving me very puzzled, for it didn't seem possible that this could happen so soon. Nevertheless, my prayer was answered in a very lovely way!

Mama, at home, had been feeling just as lonely and miserable without me, so an idea came to her. Being a hairdresser, she came to see the headmaster suggesting that she be allowed to look after the children's hair – and he agreed! Imagine my excitement the next day, seeing Mama coming into the room, throwing her arms around me, kissing me and telling me all about it. So, from then on, each time she came to the school I was able to see her! God answers prayer in such wonderful ways.

Grampy Danter and Nana Watts love me to show people what can be done through me in spite of my disability. They are very strong guides . . . and I have never known a sitting to be a failure. Sometimes, though, the guides will give me information to pass on to the sitter, which they cannot accept so they sit in front of me shaking their head, saying, "No, I'm afraid I don't understand what you mean" or "That could never happen to me."

My guides, though, will insist that what they have said will come about! So, when the sitter leaves the house, giving the impression that things have not gone well for them, I wait. Sure enough, as time passes a letter or telephone call from them will let me know how amazed they are that what was given to them had indeed come to pass . . . even though it had not seemed likely to happen in a million years.

I remember a gentleman coming to me for a private sitting. He sat before me, so nice and relaxed, handing me a brooch. Nana Watts said, "He has two more things in his pocket that you will be asked to psychometrise."

From the brooch I was able to describe many things that had happened to the owner's life, which delighted him. He then took from his jacket a flower, which Nana Watts told me had been given by him to a lady a long time ago. When she was taken ill it was passed back to him to keep for her.

As I was saying this, his eyes filled with tears; he nodded, remembering it all so clearly. After that he produced from another pocket a ring which had belonged to a dear friend and was amazed when told many details about that person's life.

With this gentleman came a lady who had psychic capabilities. As we all chatted together it became clear that she longed to develop them further. I was able to tell her without doubt that this would happen. After some brief tuition she went away very happy. Several months later the lady telephoned me to say that she had indeed begun to see spirit people, but was absolutely terrified!

Now, I simply do not understand this, for it seems so insensitive to request the co-operation of spirit guides to help in one's development and just when things begin to happen to close the door on them. Obviously, it was not right for that lady to begin this work and there were still things in her life she must experience before this could happen.

In cases like this, I recall my own impatience and always remember Grandma Thomas saying gently, "The right things will happen at the right time." And they always do.

## Chapter Twenty

## HEALING AND MEDITATION

FOR me, my healing work is the most pleasurable. Being able to ease pain and make life more comfortable for people is most rewarding. Even when someone comes to me as a last resort, after having had medical treatment for many years, healing will bring about many improvements. I receive hundreds of letters from grateful patients.

There is really no illness – or even some karmic conditions – that cannot be helped by those unidentified spiritual energies used by healers, and the evidence of this is overwhelming. These energies are able to treat mind and body. Specially trained spirit guides, some of whom have been surgeons and doctors and others who had a deep understanding of natural remedies in their own lifetime, are able to channel them through a sensitive healer, who has developed her gifts over many years.

Inside every sick person there is a free and perfect spirit, whole in every way, and this is how I see them. I do not dwell too much on their problem, but comfort and lift them up, showing them love and compassion so they are able to cope well with their particular illness.

Taking their hands in mine, and always speaking in a quiet, gentle tone to gain their confidence, gradually they will begin to relax as the healing energies do their work. Although I have had much success with many kinds of illness, my speciality is treating stroke victims, psychiatric patients and every kind of nervous disorder. People have been treated successfully by telephone. I would like to tell you about such a case.

One afternoon, a lady called Doris telephoned, asking if I could help her daughter, Ann, who had had a great deal of illness and trouble. When her husband, Derrick, passed away suddenly one year ago, she was completely devastated, becoming withdrawn, and would not even go out of the front door. Her poor mother, who was living with her, just didn't know how to cope. Ann had been a very talented teacher of music, but after Derrick's death so bad did her nervous condition become that in spite of many tablets from the doctor, all she seemed able to do was slump in an armchair in abject misery.

I spoke to Doris on the telephone for a long time, but as it was not possible to travel to see Ann I sent her a personal healing tape. Whilst doing this, Derrick appeared in my sanctuary and told me several things to tell his unhappy wife.

A day or two later, to my surprise and joy, Ann herself telephoned me hoping to hear more news about "her Derrick." On hearing her voice I knew that little Ann was psychic. Grampy Danter and Nana Watts told me that if we persevered with her condition she would be completely cured and would want to develop her gifts.

Of course, at that early stage, I did not tell her all this, but instead, when she telephoned me many, many times a week, I would talk at great length until gradually the barriers in her mind began to break down.

You see, not only am I a medium, but like to see myself as a friend, a kind of anchor. People open up to me in a way which had been impossible with their doctor or psychiatrist.

At the beginning, when looking at Ann's photograph, there were shades of dark green in her aura, showing that she was very depressed. But as the weeks passed by, and after sending healing tapes, a change in her aura began to occur. My guides explained to me that all the traumas of Ann's life had been a preparation for the psychic work she would eventually do.

Her improvement was rapid. Soon she was able to return to teaching music, so I knew that the time had come to start Ann's psychic development. During the past six months she had progressed so well it was almost unbelievable. She spends one hour a day in meditation and listening to my teaching tapes, just as Saint Saba has instructed her to do.

One day, she telephoned in great excitement, because she had seen the spirit body of her husband Derrick and various other spirit forms, which made her eager to develop further.

Every time we speak on the telephone, I find she has progressed more and more. My guide Dr Disawarra, a South African psychiatrist who had stood at my side helping me with her personal tape, nods his head and smiles his satisfaction. He died nearly nine years ago in an air disaster. Returning to South Africa from Britain for a visit, the plane blew up killing him, his wife and their two small children as well as many others who were on board.

Dr Disawarra first appeared to me a few years ago when he and his family were earthbound, and needed rescuing. I was taken through their whole horrible experience with him. Later on, he came again and wanted to assist me by putting all his knowledge of psychiatric treatment at my disposal. His help is greatly valued.

There are many people who have been helped by listening to my healing tapes. It is most important that a quiet time is set aside every day for this purpose, for in this way it will break down barriers and lift their spirits, as healing takes place.

Ann's recovery was absolute. A few days ago she telephoned, saying, "Guess what I am holding in my hand, Sally Jane?" Without giving me time to hazzard a guess, she said: "A ticket for a world cruise. I booked it and will be going in September. Alone!"

What a confident young woman she has now become . . . all because of the wonderful and patient help of my guides.

Suzette is another lady who has benefited greatly recently from spirit healing. I find it so interesting when people come to me and need a course of healing to see the gradual colour changes taking place in their aura.

The first time Suzette came for treatment it was plain to see that she was a very emotional lady. The pale red in her aura showed me that although it would take a lot to anger her, there was a very explosive side when roused. The dark green and grey illustrated there had been many illnesses and difficulties in her life – many still to be overcome. Orange in her aura shows her to be a strong personality and she had a highly intellectual nature which could be developed further.

I advised her she could be a very successful teacher and would be happy in this profession. My guides told me there were doors to be opened in her life, but she would need pushing forward gently, and this the spirit world is now doing.

Suzette is a very strong willed person and will need to be helped to overcome the hurdles ahead of her, but after several weeks' treatment the change in her aura is remarkable. I no longer see dark green and grey, only a lovely pale green which shows that healing is taking place and her health is rapidly improving, making her much more confident to go forward.

One of my guides who gives me information by means of symbols keeps showing me a bunch of keys, which always means that opportunities will soon present themselves. I look forward to being able to help her in all directions of her life, for eventually she will be a very successful and happy person. It is a very different Suzette who now enters my sanctuary with a spring in her step! I know how much my guides rejoice at the improvement in her.

In the hustle and bustle of today's materialistic world, for us to exist at all we must have a certain amount of material items for our well-being. This means a constant battle to cope for some people, and it is so very easy for them to lose their sense of direction. At some point, therefore, it becomes very necessary to meditate and reflect.

To do this, they must sit down, completely relax their limbs and learn silently to look within. This is the spiritual way to release pent-up emotions and calm troubled minds. The Chinese and Japanese have always known the value of meditation, for it is part of their culture and is widely practised today. Even in those Japanese factories in England, all employees must spend some time doing gentle relaxing exercises, designed to calm the mind and spirit before commencing their daily work. Saint Saba tells us that through meditation, people can find the Golden Key of Happiness which lies within us all.

Sadly, those who are ever striving to attain more riches and material possessions do not realise that no amount of wealth will give them an easy passage through life. The very fact that we are here on earth at this time is because there are many things which we need to experience, and then learn from those experiences, before returning once again to the spirit world. Therefore, rich or poor, life will present us with many challenges – there will be times of great joy, but also great sorrow, almost to the point of despair. The spirit way of meditation can overcome all things.

Now try the Country Cottage Meditation. Let us sit quietly relaxed, with eyes closed and visualise ourselves walking down a leafy country lane. Breathe in the sweet scent of wild honeysuckle in the air, and look closely at the delicate flowers in the hedgerows. Over on our left there are green fields dotted with sheep, as far as we can see, and which can be heard faintly bleating. The distant hills covered in purple heather make a lovely study of light and shade as the sunshine slowly sweeps across them. We gaze leisurely around at the beautiful trees with the sunshine filtering through the leaves, creating dancing patterns on the ground in front of us. The sun seems warm and comforting on our backs.

Up ahead, we catch sight of a lovely thatched cottage. Our pace quickens as we walk towards a small gate leading to a colourful garden. We stand awhile in silence, admiring this most picturesque scene. The old cottage has small diamond-paned windows, and a white painted door, framed with masses of pink roses.

We unbolt the gate – like unbolting our mind and freeing it from all discord and stress – walking slowly up the path towards the door.

Everywhere is a profusion of flowers, all blooming together, no matter if they are out of their natural season, for this is a spiritual cottage, where earthly time does not exist, only peace and harmony.

Over to our right we can see a pretty little pond and stopping awhile watch the antics of ducks, splashing about in the water. The only other sound is that of bees humming as they fly busily from flower to flower gathering pollen, and the twittering of the birds.

A cherry tree and a magnolia add the magnificence of their blossom to the perfection of it all. There is utter peace. At the white painted front door we put our key into the keyhole and unlock it, like unlocking our minds.

Inside the oak-beamed room there is a long polished refectory table with polished brass candlesticks. Seated around this table are our loved ones and friends in Spirit, waiting to greet us warmly and to help us. We feel the intensity of their love reaching out to us, and are comforted. They take our hands, urging us to sit with them. As we place our feet firmly under the table, it is like putting our life on a firm footing.

Talking with our loved ones, and listening to what the learned guides tell us, we are uplifted higher and higher and higher. When we reach a really high frequency, we move from the table over to a window, open it and look out at the wide expanse of green countryside and far off hills. We feel invigorated by the freshness and beauty for we are being given a spiritual view of how life can be opened up and cleansed.

Refreshed, we return to our friends at the table, now feeling completely able to cope with our life. For this is what life is all about – coping, coping, coping.

Allow Spirit to gather up your life and show you the way. You are a child of God and the spirit world. There is not one thing in your life that is not known, and with spirit help you can do anything good that you desire. You can be in complete control, with no more stress or anger within you. Go forward. Spirit friends will be ever at your side.

Remember too, at night, that time after time, before and during sleep, you can return to this lovely, peaceful place, and face each day with the confidence that your life will get better and better. If meditation can become part of our daily life these thought patterns will lift us to higher and higher frequencies as we are attuning our minds to the spirit world.

Have faith, and all will be well. A new pathway to life will be opened up to you.

Many times when taking a patient through meditation, their tears will flow, releasing pent up emotions, gently healing troubled minds and bodies, and easing pain. Meditation can bring a wonderful change to troubled life.

To help those people who cannot travel to my sanctuary, but want to practise meditation, I have now made some tapes available. There are also tapes for the self-healing of relief from pain.

## Chapter Twenty-One

## MY FIGHT FOR LIFE

DURING those earlier years, even though all the operations helped me to get around the rooms in our bungalow with the help of a walking aid, nobody could have foreseen how very weak my spine was to become.

When I was 33, and having yet another physiotherapy session between the parallel bars with my arms taking most of my body weight, which was quite a usual thing for me to do, it seemed much more difficult to carry out the exercises. My legs felt unable to support me. When they suddenly gave way completely I pitched forward, falling heavily.

A gentleman who was in the department waiting whilst his wife had her treatment saw what had happened and came rushing over to help me up. The physiotherapist also hurried over, saying with concern: "Whatever happened, Sally Jane? It has always been safe for me to leave you on those bars."

I did not confess to her the secret fear which had been growing within me of late, not wanting to admit even to myself that my spine was rapidly becoming weaker and weaker.

There was also something new beginning to worry me, for lately each time I had a meal, there would be a terrible sensation in my throat, which caused me to choke and have difficulty in swallowing. This was highly embarrassing one evening when friends took me out to a very nice hotel for a meal. Just when I was enjoying it all, one of the choking fits happened which alarmed my friends because they didn't know how to help, but sat looking with frightened faces until one of them put her arm around my shoulders and held my hand until the awful feeling subsided.

Of course, Mama had to be told. In the following days when eating a meal her ever-watchful eyes studied me closely. Although I made light of it, when a similar choking fit happened it was becoming harder and harder for me to conceal from her how bad things really were.

Remembering Victoria's death, the thought of going down the same road which would end my life began to fix itself in my mind. I kept all those fears to myself, hoping that these were merely temporary setbacks. However, Victoria came to me and said reassuringly: "Don't worry. You will be helped. All will be well. It is not your time. You have much work to do yet." This afforded me a certain amount of comfort.

One evening, shortly afterwards when Mama and I were meditating in my sanctuary, her guide, who, in life, was an archbishop, came to us dressed in his beautiful red robe. He is always such an imposing figure that we automatically address him as "Your Grace." He told us gently that soon it would be necessary for me to undergo a major spinal operation.

"At present," he said, "your back is curved, rather like a Bishop's crook. It must be straightened out to keep you functioning as well as allowing you to swallow normally."

Now, this came as a shock to us because up until then there had been no suggestion of this from my surgeon, so the very thought of it sent me into near panic. Mama, though, in her sensible, charming way, said: "Now look, Sally Jane, you should be quite used to having operations by now. You have always come out of them improved in some way, so if this spinal operation is necessary and can help you, you must just accept that it is for your own good, so be as brave about it as you have always been."

I knew things were deteriorating with me, that something would have to be done, and Mama talked sense.

Several weeks passed by and a bad pain began in my back, which gradually increased until it was almost unbearable. The only relief I could get from it was by sitting at the kitchen table and resting my head on it, thus taking the weight off my spine.

At the time, Dadda was feeling unwell and when young Dr Jones called at the house to see him he walked past the open kitchen door and saw me sitting like that. As he and Mama were walking upstairs, I heard Dr Jones say, "What is the matter with Sally Jane?"

Mama replied: "It's her back, doctor. She's been having such a lot of pain lately."

His response was decisive. "Well, this must not be allowed to go on, so I'll arrange an appointment for her to see a specialist at the hospital."

In no time at all, I was taken to see David Jenkins, a most kind man who explained to me that he could operate and insert two Harrrington Rods, one each side of my spine, which would straighten me up and help me to swallow normally. Only then did Mama and I realise that this would be an operation to save my life!

As Mr Jenkins was examining me, my thoughts wandered back to that other surgeon, Dr Dylan Evans, who in my younger days had carried out ten operations on my legs and hips. His great skill helped me so much. Sadly, he was struck down with a massive stroke, which paralysed him completely and took away his speech. I was remembering, shortly before his passing, when he had been brought into the physiotherapy department on a trolley, how I sat beside him feeling wretched and helpless. It seemed so sad that here was a man who had done so much for me, yet there was nothing whatever I could do to help him, except to take his cold hand and stroke his fingers, trying to convey to him my loving and sympathetic thoughts.

It left yet another great gap in my life when he passed away, but now my thoughts were brought back from those sad memories by the appearance of my old surgeon, Dylan Evans, who came and stood beside Mr Jenkins, smiling down at me saying: "Don't be afraid Poppy (his pet name for me). We will be here with the earthly surgeons."

As he spoke, the spirit form of a young Indian, Dr Hassan, also appeared. He used to be at the hospital, and I became very fond of him, but unfortunately he committed suicide which left me absolutely devastated when they told me the news. Here they were now, as solid as in life. Their presence gave me great comfort.

Arrangements were made for me to be taken to another hospital to have a lung function test to find out whether I could take the anaesthetic necessary for a lengthy operation.

All the way there in the ambulance, Dylan Evans, Dr Hassan, Grampy Danter and Nanna Watts were with me, but apart from my understandable apprehension, I was very upset because my psychic work would have to cease until my full recovery.

The operation which began early on a Friday morning took many hours. The incision made by the surgeon ran vertically along the whole length of my spine. Rods were secured by the use of a dental drill, wire and cement. Some time during the operation it was necessary for the anaesthetist to rouse me gently so I would be able to squeeze the surgeon's fingers in reply to his questions. "Can you still feel your legs?" or "Can you still feel your feet?" etc., etc.

I was vaguely aware of the surgeon's voice, telling the others present how he intended to proceed. Behind them all I could see faintly my guardian angels, standing watching as unconsciousness overcame me again.

My parents waited and waited until eventually they returned me to my bed in the small ward shared by three other ladies (the High-Dependency Unit had not yet been opened). There I lay with a drip and suction tubes attached to me, very ill indeed. Later, when slowly returning to consciousness, I became aware of a nurse using the suction pump on me and felt pain in every part of my body. A nurse would come every few hours to turn me. The very painful process of recovery began gradually.

For several weeks I lay on my back, everyone thinking what excellent progress had been made, until one evening after the visitors had all gone I felt a strange new pain in my back. Staff nurse told me: "Don't worry, it's probably the stitches pulling as they heal. I'll give you a tablet to help you sleep."

During the night, the pain became much worse, leaving me in agony. Sister brought me more tablets. The doctor on duty who usually gave me my medication could not be reached, as he had gone to a drug addiction centre to hand out drugs.

It was plain to see that staff nurse was becoming very concerned. "Try and rest, Sally Jane," she said. "The day sister will be coming on duty shortly, and she will deal with it."

As she spoke, she turned me again and blood pumped from my mouth. I had a clot on my lung!

Pandemonium broke out in the ward, as, in a kind of daze, I could hear someone calling out urgently, "Get a doctor quickly!"

But by the time one came, it was too late to take me for an X-Ray. Everything became completely unreal, as in my dream-like state the thought came to me: "Well, Sally Jane, this is it! You are about to enter the spirit world, leaving so much work unfinished." Gradually I drifted into unconsciousness. My real fight for life had begun.

However, it was not my time to die. Thankfully, after having special drugs, in four days my condition began to improve. From then on, progress was rapid, so much so that during the next few months, whilst waiting for my back to heal, the surgeon decided to operate on my legs. I was put into a "Frog" plaster again which was placed between my legs and was terribly uncomfortable. So that time it was two operations in one!

For six months I had to be in a plaster jacket from thigh to neck. At first, this had an extra support which went all around my neck and throat. The discomfort from this was almost unbearable. Even though the nurse pointed out to the doctor that she thought my neck was too short for it, he insisted it must be kept on to support my chin.

When visitors came they could see that I was very distressed, becoming blue around the face and mouth, so they told sister. When they had gone home, whichever way I tried to move, the suffocating feeling and pain could not be eased.

Dylan Evans and several other spirit doctors appeared to me saying, "You must tell them to remove this support, because there is something very wrong with it inside."

Eventually, sister brought the doctor. I said to him in no uncertain terms, "If you don't take this support off, it will choke me to death!"

He was a rather disagreeable man, and said brusquely, "Don't be silly." But in the end, he relented.

As it was being removed, both the doctor and nurse were amazed to find that a piece of plaster inside had been pressing so hard into my windpipe that it had made a hole, which was bleeding profusely. To my utter relief the chin support was not replaced!

Soon, they allowed me to go home, complete with the plaster jacket, a most bulky, unglamourous encumbrance. The next six months were dreadfully trying for Mama as it was impossible to take me out anywhere. The four walls of our house began to press in on both of us.

Towards the end of that six months' incarceration, I was beginning to be restless, wanting to carry on with my psychic work, so we restarted our meditation sessions. During one of them Saint Saba came and told us that he would be bringing another guide to join me in my future work.

"His name is Father Popperiscue, who, as a young boy of 18, decided to become a priest, feeling that he needed a life of absolute seclusion. He was unable to accept the death of his father and did not want to take on the responsibility of raising his young brother and sister. However, it soon became apparent to him that even within the monastery walls it was hard to reach the attunement and spiritual development achieved by the other monks. He did possess a psychic gift which made him aware of the spirit presence of his father, who helped him to prepare for Holy Orders." Saint Saba went on: "As you know, child, when choosing to do God's work, it is never an easy road, for there must be many tests, mentally and sometimes physically, but after many years Father Popperiscue now wishes to be of help to people on earth and has requested that I tell you of his life, and will soon join your band of workers, to instruct you in karmic readings."

Shortly afterwards, Father Popperiscue came to us, dressed in black robes. He had silver-grey hair. Since that day he has been of inestimable help to me in my work.

In his gentle voice, he is able to take people back through their past lives. These karmic readings can give a clear picture of our Cosmic Life Plan – past and present – and offer us an explanation of why our soul has chosen the life we are now living, showing us how in some cases it can be a continuation of the previous one. Many diseases and disabilities can be traced back to a previous life. Once this is interpreted it can be treated accordingly. So, with the coming of Father Popperiscue, my spiritual knowledge and development was advanced even further.

My life continued in this very uncomfortable way until it was time to have the plaster jacket taken off. And how wonderfully light my body felt without its bulky weight. I was truly elated, and totally unprepared for the blow yet to come!

Next day, my parents took me out for the first time for over six months and we went to a fête which was being opened by Ken Dodd. When he came over to speak with us we all had to laugh at his cheeky cheerful banter.

It was a happy time in spite of the fact that weakness made it impossible for me to get about without my wheelchair, but thankfully there were no more choking fits. I could hold up my head much higher, and the pain in my back was getting less and less.

So my psychic work began, and for the next 12 months continued uninterrupted. I was happy and fulfilled, but it surprised me very much, when, one night, a spirit surgeon woke me up to say: "Be warned. Do not have the operation they will suggest."

Before I could ask questions, the spirit visitor had disappeared. It left me alarmed at the possible prospect of further surgery so I tried to convince myself that it had just been a bad dream and said nothing about it to my parents.

Only a few days later I became very ill. The doctor who came to examine me took my parents out of the room, out of earshot (or so he thought) to tell them he suspected their daughter was suffering from viral meningitis. So an ambulance came and rushed me off to the hospital with terrible pains in my head.

The nurse took me into a small ante-room which to me had a distinctly cold uncomfortable atmosphere. I knew immediately that someone had very recently passed away in there and the spirit still lingered. As the nurse was putting me into bed, the spirit form of a young man was hovering by the window. He was obviously shocked and distressed, but unfortunately, in my present state, there was no way that I could help him. Grampy Danter came to say: "Don't worry. Soon you'll be moved from here."

Almost as he spoke another nurse came bustling into the room, saying: "Sorry love, but I'll have to move you. There is a lady in a coma who has just been brought in. She needs absolute quiet."

After many tests, the following day, a doctor came to me and said, "It is not meningitis, but the after-effect of your spinal operation."

He was such a nice young man, who seemed so sorry to have to tell me that if the pain continued it might be necessary to have neurosurgery – a neck fusion which in some cases is not very successful. I sensed a danger at once . . . for this is what the spirit surgeon had warned me about a few weeks previously.

"Do you mean that it is possible for me to end up like a cabbage?" I asked him.

He replied quickly, "Of course, there are never any guarantees, but we must try to relieve your pain."

My prompt answer was, "Now that you have told me the risk, no thank you." Jokingly, I added, "Perhaps, you had better go back to the drawing-board."

However, after giving me many strong pain-killing tablets which worked very well I was allowed to return home with a large supply of them.

Alas, after a few weeks it all started again with a vengeance one night, the pain becoming intense. Mama came rushing into my bedroom when she heard my groans to give me some pain-killers and stayed with me until morning, with neither of us getting much sleep. I begged her not to get the doctor, for it would mean my going back into hospital for the dreaded operation.

When the pain became almost too much to bear, Nanna Watts came, bringing with her the healer John Cain, whom we had met years ago at Stansted Hall.

"Sally Jane, do you remember me?" he asked. "I promised you I would come if you needed me. Now listen, leave off all those strong medications except for the anti-inflammatory drugs. Try to relax while I give you healing."

Mama, who could also see and hear John, listened to what he was telling us, perhaps wondering about the wisdom of it, but nevertheless did as he said and withheld what should have been the next dose of tablets. Gradually, the dreadful pain began to ease, enabling me to drift into a long, peaceful sleep.

When waking up the next day, my head felt clear, with no pain at all. I cried out to John in thankfulness, even though he was no longer there, knowing that he had indeed saved me from having neurosurgery from which it was possible I would not have survived.

Having now recovered from all that, work continued in earnest. With my advertisement once again in "Psychic News," phone calls and letters came from many parts of the UK and overseas, so I was very busy indeed.

Days, weeks and months passed smoothly. There were several check-ups at the hospital. During the last one of these, just before Christmas, the surgeon told me that a tendon operation was necessary on my hands, but as it was not too urgent there might be a delay before it could be done.

Christmas Eve arrived. We were all looking forward to a few days' holiday at this lovely time. Mama was lifting me out of my wheelchair, when we heard a loud "ping." One of my back rods had rejected! This meant immediate surgery to replace it. So I had to go off to hospital again, spending the holiday, after the operation, in the very festive-looking ward with its Christmas tree and decorations.

The doctors and nurses did their utmost to bring us good cheer in spite of everything. One of the surgeons brought each person a present. There was a lovely atmosphere in the ward. I progressed well.

It was a few weeks afterwards that the surgeon came to my bedside, sat down and said: "We are so pleased we have been able to help you, Sally Jane. The rods should be fine now for quite a while, but," he paused and took my hand, "I must explain, that in a few years they will need to be replaced with another kind of rod, a Lukie Rod. This will be permanent!"

The news took me aback somewhat, as it was a dreadful thought that I would have to go through all that agony again. However, the realisation that my life depended on it somehow brought me a kind of calm acceptance – whatever was necessary would have to be done, like it or not, but I was always very grateful to the surgeons who were able to help me. They, too, were pleased to be able to do so.

I very often think about another surgeon who operated on my leg when I was about 16 years old – such a skilled, kind and compassionate man, yet having to bear a great tragedy with his own family. I was telling Mama how very kind that surgeon had been to me.

"Yes," she said, "but what a sad life he had. One of the nurses told me that all four of that poor man's children were born mentally and physically handicapped, giving constant anxiety to him and his wife. In spite of him being such a skilled surgeon there is nothing he can do for them."

It saddened me so much to hear about this. Later, after lights out, I asked Saint Saba, "Why is such a good and compassionate man made to suffer in that way?"

He said, "My child, it is his karma, chosen by him long ago, to help the progression of his soul."

I interrupted him, feeling very angry. "But why did it have to be all four of his children? Surely one handicapped child is enough to bring up and deal with. Four are too many."

Patiently, Saint Saba smiled kindly at my outburst. "Yes, yes, little one, he has chosen a severe test, but is a man quite equal to the task, and will bear his life bravely."

Some months later I heard that the surgeon's little daughter had passed away and the rest of the family had gone to live in America.

It was years later that my next operation was carried out, the Harrington Rods removed and replaced by the Lukie Rods which have remained in my back ever since. Fortunately, it was not necessary for me to be put into a complete plaster jacket this time. Whilst waiting for the scar from this to heal the surgeon carried out the tendon operation on my hands.

People often tell me that I have good sense of humour and I must admit to being able always to see the funny side of life. One incident at the time of those last two operations really did cause me a lot of amusement. There was poor old me in my hospital bed, trussed up like a mummy, barely able to move, with both hands and arms bandaged up to the elbows, when early one morning, a young new nurse came into the ward and said cheerfully: "Good morning, love, Here's your wash-bowl and toilet bag, so get on with it for it's nearly breakfast time." With that she breezed off up the ward!

Looking at the bowl of water on the bed-table in front of me and turning my head painfully towards Betty in the next bed who had begun to wash herself, our eyes met. She took one look at me and seeing my predicament, and the impossibility of my being able to do anything to help myself, we both saw the funny side of it and burst out laughing so loudly that everyone began to stare. The nurse came back to see what the joke was, realised immediately her mistake, blushed with embarrassment and stammered: "Oh dear, sorry. Just didn't think."

Quickly busying herself with the flannel and soap she began to do the job for me. Several times during the day Betty and I couldn't contain our giggles when we thought about it.

A few nights later a terrible feeling of danger came over me when I suddenly awoke – a danger from fire with the choking smell of smoke seeming to be everywhere, filling my lungs. None of the nurses appeared to notice anything amiss, so I assumed it was a dying bonfire in the grounds and took no more notice of it.

Early in the morning there seemed to be a panic going on, with nurses pushing beds out of the ward. One came hurrying over to me saying: "Don't be afraid, Sally Jane. A bomb warning has been sent to the hospital. We must evacuate everyone as soon as possible."

People in the immediate vicinity were also warned to vacate their homes until the bomb could be located – men, women and children were milling about in their nightclothes! Staff nurse had tucked up a little girl patient at the end of my bed so it wouldn't do for her to see my fear, but Grampy Danter, Nanna Watts and Frankie appeared giving me assurance that nothing bad would happen.

Apparently, the news of the bomb scare soon spread. Friends, worried about me, got into their car and speeded towards the hospital to find out if everyone was safe. On the way, they were in an accident with another car on a similar mission. However, detectives discovered two youths in the grounds who admitted they had done it for a joke.

What a panic it caused!

Afterwards, safely back in the ward, with my friends beside my bed, one told me: "I've ruined the side of my car, Sally Jane, but you are much more important to us. When we heard about the bomb scare on the radio we couldn't get here quickly enough."

So my psychic warning had alerted me to a dangerous situation which could have resulted in fire, but happily it was averted.

As usual, when my convalescence was progressing well, people in the hospital began to ask if I would help them, which I did gladly. It always amazes me how quickly the word gets around about my psychic work and how quickly it snowballs, which proves how very much a medium's work is needed in this life. My body has been made imperfect with the many scars from all the operations I have had to undergo, but because of my God-given gifts all this counts as nothing when there is His work to be done. One has only to go into a physiotherapy department to realise how much people suffer.

One afternoon, when having my treatment, I met a poor gentleman, very tall in stature, who was in such pain that he was almost cracking up under it. He began to weep, so I asked the nurse to push my wheelchair over to him and began to offer words of comfort, taking both his hands in mine. As the healing energies began to flow into him, he looked at me surprised and confused, and said: "You are comforting me. But you're in a worse state than I am and you're only a little slip of a thing."

We began to talk and he told me about his two young children, how desperately worried he was about providing for his family for the future.

Sister Dominique appeared beside him, explaining to me that in spite of his present condition, in time he would find a very lucrative position, but would need to persevere and be patient.

The man then said: "Are you by chance one of these spiritual healers? Since you took my hands, believe it or not, this awful pain is leaving me. I don't understand!"

So then was the time to tell him about all my gifts and also what Sister Dominique had told me about his future. The change in him was immediate.

"That's absolutely wonderful," he said with delight. "I just can't wait to tell my wife about you."

It was quite amazing to see the relief on his face, for hope had been given to him which would help greatly with his recovery. At such times as this, when my guides feel it necessary for the well-being of a patient they allow me to give people a further view of their life, the comfort it brings to them and the joy to me is something very precious. I promised to give him absent healing every night, knowing that it would help him in the long fight which had just begun – a fight that he would win.

On another occasion, a young man of 18 was brought in for physiotherapy. He had become a partial paraplegic in an accident when diving from the pier into the sea, crashing his head against a submerged rock. It was almost impossible for him to come to terms with this crippling condition and was obvious that he considered life for him was over. Sue, the physiotherapist, confided to me: "I don't quite know what to do, Sally Jane. If only he would try to co-operate, especially now that there is some movement in his fingers. Do you think you could talk to him?"

Sue pushed my wheelchair over to where he sat, looking angry and frustrated.

"What's the good of all this physiotherapy?" he said. "No one is going to want me like this, so I might as well be dead. There can't be a God or He wouldn't allow me to suffer like this."

He ranted and raved as Sue brought him a cup of milk and tried to place his fingers around it.

"Come along now, try to hold this up to your mouth. You can do it," she told him encouragingly. He became very aggressive indeed, shouting "Take it away!"

Poor Sue looked at me despairingly, so I took the cup in my hand and tried to persuade him to hold it.

"If you try to make me drink that, I'll spit it all out," he stormed.

"All right then," I said, "if that will make you happy."

This seemed to make him see red. So angry was he that his fingers gripped the cup tightly. Filling his mouth with the milk, he spat it out all over me! His anger had given him the impetus which put him one step towards recovery.

"Oh, it's all right for you," he said to me. "You don't have to be helped in and out of bed like a baby." This made me laugh quietly.

"I'm afraid I do, but we both still have a brain, don't we?"

He calmed down then and began asking me about my disability. Sue came over to us and said, "Tell him about your work, Sally Jane." As I began to explain it all the young man showed such interest that his questions came thick and fast.

Each time we met in the department having treatment, he would want me to tell him more and more. Sue took me to one side, saying: "He has begun to show a lot of improvement, Sally Jane. Now that he is co-operating, we will be able to help him a lot."

So, even when my course of physiotherapy came to an end and I did not see him again, it was clear that as my guides had told me, he realised that having a disability was not the end!

A few years ago, when travelling home in the ambulance, I had a very frightening experience. My wheelchair came unfastened in the hydraulic lift and I was pitched onto the floor of the ambulance. A few moments before it happened a terrible feeling of fear swept over me and Frankie appeared, but almost immediately the accident occurred.

"Oh my God, my rods must surely have been damaged," I thought, feeling very angry with the young ambulance driver as he knelt beside me.

"Quickly," I panicked. "Get me back to hospital. I hope to goodness it doesn't mean my having to go through that awful operation again."

At that, Grampy Danter appeared and said soothingly: "Now, now angel, don't upset yourself. There is no damage, though you are bruised and shaken. Everything will be all right."

The young driver was terribly upset and after covering me gently with a blanket, got back into the ambulance and made a phone call. Shortly afterwards another ambulance and crew arrived and took me back to the hospital where the surgeon confirmed exactly what Grampy Danter had said.

"You were very lucky my dear," he told me. "I understand that you missed hitting your head by inches, which might have been very serious indeed."

All the time the surgeon was speaking Frankie stood beside me and winked at me in his usual way as if to say "Protecting you is what I'm here for" as he has done on so many other occasions.

So you see, I'm never, ever, completely alone.

*Chapter Twenty-Two*

## MORE SPIRIT PROOF

THE first time nurses lifted me gently out of bed into my wheelchair after the spinal operation, no matter how carefully I tried to ease myself this way or that there seemed to be no way of finding a more comfortable and less painful position. It made me wonder if this was how it would be for the rest of my life.

"You must just persevere, Sally Jane, until you find the best way of sitting," they told me. And so it turned out, for it was surprising how quickly I found my best position for longer and longer periods of time.

Meanwhile, treatment continued on my hands. Even though it was obvious that my general progress would be slow, one afternoon during treatment I was totally unprepared for the shock I received when asking the physiotherapist, "How long will it be before trying my walking aid again?"

She looked at me in surprise and replied shortly, "Surely you've been told it will be *impossible* for you ever to walk again."

I could not believe my ears, for it had never occurred to me that this might be the case. The physiotherapist, seeing my distress, said more gently: "Your body and legs have become too weak to carry your weight. But at least the back is much straighter, and now you can swallow normally." I felt too stunned to reply.

Back home, tears rolled down my cheeks when telling my parents all about it. Thumping the armrest of my wheelchair in fury I raged, "How can it possibly have been worth going through all those operations and pain, just to end up like this?"

Mama and Dadda didn't know what to say to comfort me, but later, when in bed, they both came and sat in my room for a long time, until I fell into a fitful sleep.

During the night, Saint Saba, Grampy Danter and Nanna Watts came. I asked them, "Why must it be like this for me?"

Saint Saba replied in his usual gentle way. "Child, you have now entered another phase of your karma which must be borne patiently, but do not think that it will interfere with your work for God. No, not at all. Rather, it will continue more than ever before."

I listened miserably to his words as he went on, "Some time in the future you will meet someone who will write a book about you and your work which will be a great inspiration to many people."

This news seemed most improbable at the time, for the last operations had left me virtually helpless, with my hands too weak to even hold a pen! However, on reflecting more deeply about this, what Saint Saba had said made sense – that if a book was going to be written, then someone else could possibly do it. But who? The whole idea, while seeming remote, at least gave me something to stimulate my imagination. Once again, I began to look forward.

My surgeon, David Jenkins, has told me that now there is nothing more he can do for my spine, and that most probably small operations on various parts of my body will become necessary from time to time.

Gradually, I have resigned myself to becoming wheelchair-bound, totally reliant upon Mama's help for my day-to-day care. Both my parents help me in my work, by opening envelopes for me, addressing letters and sending off tapes. You can see, therefore, how well blessed I have been by being born into such a wonderful family who make it possible for my work to continue.

Saint Saba was right, as always. My work *has* gone on, and in such a way that sometimes there are just not enough hours in the day, but it makes me very happy that so many people have been given such wonderful proof of spirit existence.

Sometimes, when reading a person's aura, they will say, "Oh, Sally Jane, how I wish that I could see what you see."

So I was overjoyed when one morning during my meditation, Saint Saba appeared, bringing with him a white-haired French gentleman, with brown eyes and Jacob's beard, wearing an old fashioned top hat and long cloak.

"This is Edmund Dantes, who many years ago was part of your family line, and he would like to teach you how to prepare auragraphs," he told me.

Now, the first time I had ever seen one of these was years ago at Stansted Hall, when a medium handed me one saying, "What can you read from this?" My interpretation proved to be absolutely correct!

An auragraph is a circular drawing, showing the various colours in a person's aura, also depicting, by way of pictures and symbols, many aspects of their life, health, emotions, character, their present state of spiritual development and psychic capabilities. A medium is able to draw these, giving an in-depth interpretation of it all, so that a sitter can indeed see what the medium sees. It is quite fascinating and brings an added dimension to my work.

More and more people were coming to me for advice about their psychic development.

A young lady named Pauline sent me some photographs, from which I was able to analyse her life and the fact that she very much wanted to become a healer. After this, she telephoned to ask for a private sitting.

When she arrived, Mama showed her into my sanctuary. Pauline was such a sweet-natured girl. As we sat chatting over a cup of tea there seemed such a lovely rapport between us that it felt as if we had known each other all our lives. Her aura contained many beautiful colours, but showed despondency, caused by her feeling that she would never be able to find answers to what she was seeking.

"Sally Jane," she said, "I really don't know how to develop my psychic capabilities. Development circles seem to have done nothing but confuse me and get me nowhere. Can you help?"

As I looked at her eager face it saddened me to know how many people there are, just like her, capable of doing great things, yet not knowing how to reach their potential. I deplore the fact that some development circles take these delicate young novices and fail to give them proper guidance.

"Well," I assured her, "you will become a very good healer, but you must be thoroughly dedicated, and sit for meditation every day after fasting. In this way, you will reach the inner spiritual goal of life more easily." Another reason for fasting is because if food is consumed beforehand, some of the taste will remain in the mouth, making it impossible to recognise a "psychic taste" or smell when it is given by Spirit and could be evidential.

As I was saying this to Pauline, there was a guru standing beside her, telling me how to explain things. I took both her hands and my guides gathered all around us. Almost immediately I saw black, murky water, icebergs and a ship with the name "Titanic" written on the side. A little boy appeared standing close to me and said, "My name is Patrick."

When I told Pauline about him she said: "Oh, Sally Jane, I have often 'seen' the 'Titanic' and a lady dressed in blue. Do you see her?"

I replied, "No, but there is a little boy here called Patrick, who is telling me that before the voyage his mother had made him a suit out of one belonging to his father."

Obviously, he was earthbound, and had been so ever since he drowned in the disaster. He needed rescuing badly. I slipped into trance and felt his little hand taking mine and drawing me down into the cold, dark water, showing me how he and his father, who was on the lower deck, perished together with his grandmother and baby sister. There was debris and people threshing about in the darkness.

Patrick took me all over the ship, showing me how the tragedy happened. I could see that many people couldn't possibly have got out of the hell down there. He told me that his grandmother had pressed a tiny gold cross and a rosary into his hand, but then they were all separated in the confusion.

"I was so frightened," he said. "When I entered the spirit world, my father, grandmother and baby sister were waiting for me, but the shock of it all kept drawing me back to where it all happened."

At this, his mother named Bridget appeared, dressed in dark blue, with a knitted shawl around her shoulders. She was so excited at getting back her son that she took his hand and thanked me profusely for having rescued him. Bridget went on to tell me that they had all lived in Dublin originally and were very poor. They had been taking the sea voyage to another land in the hope of finding a better life for the family.

Of course, the "Titanic" tragedy happened many years ago. After being rescued by me, Patrick vanished for a short time and reappeared looking the way he actually is now, having grown and reached his prime, which is the way of the spirit world. He told us he would like to stay with Pauline and help throughout her development.

I said to Pauline, "We can begin now by doing 'The Cottage Meditation'," and began to take her through it gently, but after a while she interrupted me, saying rather sorrowfully, "I'm sorry, Sally Jane, but something inside me seems to block things somehow."

At this, Nana Watts and Patrick's grandmother became rather impatient, because they knew that only a little push was needed to open the psychic door of Pauline's true life pattern.

When people learn how to develop their psychic gifts the correct way, it can bring untold joy. I love teaching would-be mediums because they are the future links between our world and the next; each one must be tutored carefully and thoroughly. It is always necessary to stress that in this work there are no short cuts. Development must take place in gradual stages, for in this way they reach the highest vibrations. When people are called "to do God's work," He gives them the inner strength to do so and finally, when they reach their goal, helping many people, it is then they find real fulfilment and pleasure for there lies the Golden Key to happiness.

During years of working with Spirit, I have seen and heard so much about the many tragedies which befall our fellow human beings. In my own home there are many boxes of "Thank you" letters sent to me by grateful people, who have been given wonderful evidence from Spirit, that death is most certainly not the end of our life or those who have gone before.

Some of the letters affect me deeply, especially those from people who want to tell the world how much Spirit has helped them.

I remember a few years ago, a young couple Seline and Charles Goulding coming for a private sitting, after being so impressed with the results of a taped reading received by their agnostic friend from me. They "just had to see Sally Jane for ourselves!"

This lovely young couple sat before me, waiting eagerly to hear what I would tell them. Looking at their auras was pure delight for me, for never before had I come across two more equally matched. The colours blended perfectly showing me that this was one of those marriages "made in heaven" which would be a long and happy one. Aura-matching is so important for harmony, no matter what the circumstances.

I began by telling them that they had been together in a previous life – their names, where they lived and many details about that life. Smiling with excitement, both confirmed everything that another medium had previously told them.

Seline's mother appeared close by her side. When I described her to them, passing on her messages, the great joy on both their faces made me quite emotional. During our long sitting and the conversation afterwards, they asked me about healing. I told them about my own experience with healing from John Cain.

Before leaving my home, they thanked me profusely for "all I had done for them" and even though they were leaving the country to go to live in Australia, Seline and Charles promised to keep in touch. Some months later a letter arrived from them enclosing a long article which had appeared in an Australian newspaper about me and my work. It was indeed a glowing report which touched me deeply.

Then there was the wonderful letter from a gentleman who signed himself "R. Cash" which I include in its entirety:

Dear Sally,

I am enclosing a long statement regarding your excellent clairvoyancy and give you full permission to use all, or any part of it, as you choose for this is to testify as to the accuracy and truth of spirit communication from the spirit world through your mediumship and the loving help from your guides.

On Easter Sunday, April 6, 1980, I lost the most precious and beautiful thing to me on earth – her name was Ann. The list of her attributes is endless – she had beauty, wisdom, charm, a sense of humour, was always considerate of others, and, in fact, to me was an absolute angel.

My tragic loss devastated me utterly and completely. I could see no point in anything, no longer seeing reason for life. God had forsaken me and my soul felt empty. I shed many tears during the following months, wandering, hopelessly lost.

However, as time went by, very gradually reason began to return, and questions started to stir deeply within my consciousness. Why are we here? Why do we love? Is there a God, a loving God, who understands love and all the pleasures of life? Surely Fate alone could not be the Scene, the be-all and end-all of everything!

Things began to change within me. I had dreams of my lovely Ann still being there, smiling and happy, whispering to me, kissing my lips and holding my hand. Was I finally going mad, driven to morbid despair? Looming on the horizon were thoughts of my having to enter a mental institution. Truth had to be found. Was Ann still alive somewhere in another world? Could proof of her survival be found? Could there really be a God, a Divine Light, a System, a Law? Has man a dual nature, a spirit being encased in a physical body, incarnated on earth to learn lessons in order to evolve?

Reading through my mother's psychic weekly newspaper, I saw an advertisement which started my interest. I went to see a medium at the Greater World Christian Spiritualist Association. At the time I was still very confused, but evidence was there. How could the sweet lady medium know the things she told me? Doubts crept in as I thought, "Can she be reading my mind?"

It was some time before I began to cope with life again, and eventually realised the true value of that sitting. I thought if I sent away for a taped reading, a medium would not have my physical presence, and would know nothing about me, apart from my request for a postal reading.

Again I found an advertisement, a medium living in Wales, miles away from my home and it seemed ideal. So off went my letter to Sally Jane Danter. A week or two went by, and sure enough, when I came home from work one day there was a reply. I listened intently and kept re-listening to the information which proved, beyond any doubt, that continuation of life exists for my darling Ann. The intimate truths of what Sally Jane told me was outstanding.

Special attention was given to the manner of Ann's passing, a sudden, swift, horrific accident. Sally Jane wrote, "I feel a sudden bump and such pains in my head, as if it is breaking to pieces – disintegrating."

Ann and I had been out horse riding and were resting awhile. She got back into the saddle, and I was just passing the riding hat to her when something shot out of the hedge, which startled the horses, who galloped madly down the road, skidded on some loose gravel and catapulted Ann up into the air. I ran down the road, found her lying face down, and as I turned her over, saw that her mouth, nose and ears were pouring with blood.

Weeks later, the coroner told us that Ann had died of multiple compression fractures to the skull.

All this Sally Jane described to me. Reference was also made to the lining of the coffin, pale pink, which was correct.

Regarding the photograph of Ann I sent to Sally Jane, she said on tape, "I don't see her as she appears on this photograph, as she is now, wearing her hair up, and is wearing a crucifix." All true. In the photograph I sent, Ann had dark hair, but some years later, she tinted her hair "honey blonde" and in one of my favourite photographs of her she has her hair up and tied at the back. As for the crucifix, Ann always wore one, and after the accident, this was the only thing that was given to us.

Sally Jane told me that symbolically I must hold on to Ann's hand, for she would always be there to guide me. This was so evidential, because whenever we went out walking or shopping, Ann would always hold my hand.

Sally Jane also told me that Ann was very methodical, very strong and level headed, always neatly dressed in dark colour clothes, and used a lovely perfume; indeed she was a precious jewel of a lady. All these things were so true, for Ann did love black, it was her favourite, and she had bottles and bottles of perfume, and took special care of her clothing so as to look neat.

These things proved to me beyond doubt, that my precious, beautiful Ann is there in Spirit. She has lost none of her personality and character, with the same loving bond, never to be broken.

This is all the absolute truth.

R. Cash.

So you see, that this is just one of thousands of cases which proves that love never dies. Ann's love for her young man will continue for ever. Through Spirit help two young people were re-united.

Now here is a tribute from a gentleman called Michael:

This is to thank Sally Jane Danter for all the help she has given me.

My wife, Jennifer, went to the doctor with a small lump on the leg which he diagnosed as a sebaceous cyst. Over a period of time she had four small operations which entailed cutting into the leg to remove it. It did not heal. After a while my wife went to see him again. Rather than have yet another operation, she asked if she could have a second opinion.

The specialist whom she saw had her admitted to the hospital that very day. After a biopsy, it turned out to be a malignant carcinoma. An operation was performed, after which I was told by the specialist that Jennifer had only a month to live.

This was a very traumatic experience. I found it extremely difficult to cope with the situation, but we just carried on daily. My wife is a very strong person and said, "We'll fight this thing" and how we did!

A friend advised us to see a faith healer in Worthing, Jack Hoad, who started to treat her. I must say that he was marvellous, and Jennifer always felt better after treatment at Jack's home. She said that he did more for her than all the doctors. We would go to him every week and it seemed that the trouble had been cured: things were looking up. Jennifer was always in good spirits, never complained, but just fought.

In July, about nine months later, the whole thing flared up again, this time by-passing the leg and affecting the hip. This was the end for her.

When my wife died, I was absolutely shattered. If you have a straightforward illness and die, there is not much you can do about it, but with something like this, it seemed that so much time had been lost in carrying out her treatment. Apart from that, she always seemed so fit before and was never ill, in spite of being so hard working. This made it so terribly hard to take for me.

I had already been reading a lot of books that Jack Hoad gave me to read which I found very comforting, particularly one by Silver Birch, an Indian guide, called "The Teachings of Silver Birch." I had read all Doris Stokes' books and many others, but wanted to read many more and wrote to "Psychic News" for a book list, and a free copy of "Psychic News," which was very interesting.

By this time I had a strange urge to contact a medium, but wanted a private sitting. A letter to Doris Collins brought me no reply, which was understandable for she must get thousands of such requests.

However, in "Psychic News" there was an article about Sally Jane Danter, and also her advertisement, so I decided to write to her, enclosing a photograph and one of my wife's necklaces. In due course, back came the taped sitting, which proved to be most helpful and comforting. I have since had three private sittings with Sally Jane, which have also helped me so much. It is remarkable how many of the things she tells me nobody but myself could possibly have known. In many cases, much of what she has told me has transpired. There is no doubt at all that some people are born with psychic gifts and Sally Jane is certainly one of them.

Jennifer and I were married for 18 years, and we were very close partners in marriage and business. Nobody could have had a finer wife. That is why her death has been rather like climbing up a high hill of misery.

I play Sally Jane's taped recordings over an over again and they have given so much strength in lots of ways. There was no one else to turn to and when this sort of situation occurs; all that a person longs for is some kind of message from the one they have loved and lost. Just to know that wherever they may be, all is well with them. When a medium is able to do this, it means such a lot. I thank God that we have been given a medium like Sally Jane. She helped me through a time when the bottom of my world really dropped out.

Thank you, Sally Jane, I will keep in close touch with you in future years. Keep up the good work!

After a sitting with me, Michael telephoned to say that he had a strange experience at his home. He had been sitting alone in his kitchen, where high above on an oak beam there hung a copper kettle. As he watched it began to move. There was no draught in the room to cause the movement, yet it kept swinging backwards and forwards for some time.

He was so amazed that he telephoned me to ask me what it could possibly be. I was able to tell him that his wife was trying to draw his attention, to tell him she was there.

Sometimes, if we cannot see the spirits of our loved ones they will actually move things so as to catch our eye.

Michael has asked that his message be included in this book. He is a very kind and gentle man. I find it a privilege to work for him and will continue to do so as long as he needs me.

Not long ago, a lady and her daughter came for a private sitting which not only proved evidential to them, but most intriguing for me, because shortly afterwards they brought me the very articles shown me by Spirit to prove identity.

During the sitting, an elderly white haired lady, who said that her name was Lizzie, appeared. Standing close beside the elder of the two ladies who was her daughter. Lizzie, a strong forceful character, told me many things that had happened during her life. She had always worked hard in a fish and chip shop, but passed away quickly after a stroke.

When I described her in detail, passing on all the information she gave me, her daughter and granddaughter exclaimed in delight, "That's exactly how she was!"

Then Lizzie showed me an exquisite crochet-work bedspread, more beautiful even than that I had seen in Bruges. This, she explained, had been made by her first as a bedspread, but was altered later to be used as a tablecloth. She then helped to reunite her daughter through me with several other sadly-missed members of the family.

A few days later, when they brought the crochet tablecloth for me to see, it was exactly as shown to my by Spirit. Because Lizzie was so grateful to me for reuniting her with the family she asked to work with me, and is now a very strong guide.

I first made the acquaintance of Doreen Hedges, when she wrote to me requesting a postal taped reading. As soon as I held in my hand the photograph she had enclosed, it was clear to me that here was a very loving, generous, kind lady. She had been a nursing sister in many hospitals.

Very soon, as I worked, her husband Joe appeared. He passed with a stroke. I described him as he sat in a wheelchair, white haired and with thick rimmed spectacles.

Doreen's father in Spirit also came. He had a strong Cockney accent and during his lifetime suffered much.

"Please tell my Tinkerbell (his pet name for Doreen) that she must go forward with her psychic development," he said.

Joe was also anxious for me to tell his wife that she must pick up where she left off over 25 years ago. Doreen had sat in a development circle, but seemed unable to make any progress. I knew it had been the wrong atmosphere for her there, because other sitters had different vibrations and ideals.

After hearing the messages from her father and husband, she asked me if she could become one of my students so I agreed to send her some personal instruction tapes.

At first, Doreen found it difficult to fast before meditating because she suffers from scoliosis, is in a wheelchair and on pain-killing medicines, but we worked out that the best time for her would be later in the evening. Soon she settled down to a regular routine and is now developing well.

Her sister, Daphne, also had a nursing career, became interested and sent for a taped sitting. She was delighted when I was able to reunite her with her husband, Bernie, who passed suddenly. He told me many things about their lives, and the plans they had made for the future.

As sisters, they are both kind and gentle, but Doreen is the more outgoing of the two, though each will become a very good healer. They telephone me every other day, as well as putting all their experiences on tape to send me monthly.

I like my students to tell me everything they see, sense, hear and to describe it all in detail, thus checking on them at every stage. I always feel that not enough time is spent in doing this, for how else can they achieve the high standard of mediumship, which is so hard to find?

The most amazing thing to me is that Doreen has a Red Indian guide called Cochise, who many years ago met one of my guides, "Silver

Lily" of Cochise's tribe, when they were having what the Indians call a pow-wow for peace. Doreen has written a little book about her past lives and was astounded to learn about the connection between her guide and mine. It proves how often links with our past lives are introduced again in a present one.

The development of both sisters is progressing steadily. My experience is that lady students seem to forge ahead faster than gentlemen. No doubt this is because one needs to be absolutely dedicated, fasting and meditating at the same time every day. Probably other commitments in a man's working life prevent this.

It has been possible for me to take Doreen back over several of her previous lives. In early historic times, she had a mother who was a medicine-woman, treating people with herbs. When the old lady died, her daughter (Doreen) took over her mother's craft. Because she was not fully trained, this caused a tragedy for when treating some members of her family she made a terrible mistake by giving them poisonous herbs which killed them.

In a later life, she was a nurse in the Boer War at the time of Florence Nightingale – and the conditions were appalling.

Doreen's other lives show how very often conditions and experiences repeat themselves life after life, in her case, always involving nursing and medicine.

Now here is a letter from Doreen:

It is a pleasure to put into words my perception of Sally Jane Danter and her work. I knew nothing concerning her until a few weeks ago, when I read an article in "Psychic News."

The fact that she is confined to a wheelchair impressed me above all else because, you see, I have nursed those who are disabled, and therefore understand as far as it is possible to do so when one is fully active, what problems they have to face, and since looking after my husband following a severe stroke, until his death.

Time passed. I kept thinking, "I must contact Sally Jane," and eventually did. Before making any comments on that, I would have to say that I have always been aware of the spirit world and how they work, or so I thought, and at one time realised that I had the ability to be used as a channel for healing, mainly for animals, and was clairvoyant and clairaudient. I thought that that was all there was to know.

In the stress of the following 25 years of personal problems and illness, all my psychic capabilities went into a state of limbo, even though they were still there. I sent for many psychic readings, but always felt, when I received the replies, as if I could have done better than that myself.

On receiving Sally Jane's taped reply, a new life opened up for me. You see, I am now disabled. All that was in my mind was, "I'm not even 60 years old and I'm on the scrap-heap." Sally told me that my infirmity cannot be removed, but can be greatly helped by spiritual healing. I understood so much more when she explained that we all choose the life we will live, when we are reborn on this earth, and this is our karmic pattern. Long before I knew anything about Sally Jane and her work I had had the privilege of being regressed to three of my former lives.

Working as she does from her wheelchair, Sally Jane is indeed one of God's gifts to creation. Her words of guidance have given me back a purpose in life. I feel as if I have been brought out into the light, out of a dark, dark, fell. Although life will still have its problems for me, I am now like a prisoner set free.

Sally Jane is a beautiful soul. Her voice and purity radiate out from each tape. Her clairvoyance is, as far as I'm concerned, unsurpassed, as indeed is her healing gift. Added to all this is her ability to teach the correct way of spiritual development and the beauty and love that is pouring into her from the spirit world. I have no doubt whatsoever that she is the most able and compassionate of workers that God, through his spirit guides, could have to lead his earthly children onto the right path.

I have always had a split-second build-up of spirit people and places, but through Sally Jane's tuition I am now learning to read the aura in all its beauty. She has assured me that I will see spirit beings just as clearly as I see earthly people, and will understand the true meaning of symbols given by spirit guides.

Sally Jane has also sent me my karmic reading, which along with other lives, relates details of myself in early historic times, a fact I had always suspected, but of which I had no proof.

This is just a small part of all the knowledge she is able to teach. My final word is that Sally Jane is a star among satellites.

Here is another letter, this is one from a lady called Ann in Wolverhampton:

Last August I contacted Sally Jane Danter after seeing her advert and a lovely piece about her in "Psychic News."

Since having my first tape off her she has gone on to help me in so many, many wonderful ways.

She has my Derick, who passed into Spirit from brain tumours, in her sanctuary, and he tells me things via Sally Jane. She heals me. I have made so much progress from a nervous illness and the bereavement with her. Nothing seems too much trouble for her, in spite of her own problems. I have had, and still have, wonderful tapes to help me in my spiritual development – psychic sittings and healing tapes, lovely chat tapes! We are firm friends! The support I have had over many 'phone calls to her is just out of this world.

I feel I wouldn't be in this positive and uplifted frame of mind were it not for Sally Jane. Such kindness is rare these days. My agoraphobia of 30 years has vanished, my confidence restored. My self-esteem and much more have been allowed to take the place of a fearful, rather negative and depressed lady. All of what I write is truly a plain fact. I am still going from strength to strength! This is especially terrific because of the extreme pain this lovely lady works with. She is such an example to us all, I expect; certainly this is so for me.

I long to take her pain away, but of course I can't, so I pray and hope for her and feel "Let her be an inspiration to you Ann," so her own extreme suffering is this most certain example and inspiration to me.

Letters like these are most precious to me. However, very occasionally someone will send for a postal reading with the sole intention of trying to catch me out! At such times, I am very glad of my sense of humour.

For instance, I had a letter signed by a lady, who also enclosed a picture of herself. Soon after beginning her reading, Diane came to me and said, "This is not a lady, it is a man."

Switching off my tape recorder, I again studied the photograph and said to her: "You must be mistaken, Diane. Look the lady is here in this picture."

Diane, though, still insisted that it was a man, so I simply continued with the reading as if to a lady and left it at that.

By a strange coincidence, many months later, the truth of the matter came to light, showing me that Diane had been right.

Sometimes, it happens in reverse, and a lady will hide behind a man's name, not realising that this can't fool Spirit.

Another time, a husband and wife called to see me. The lady handed me one of her mother's bedroom slippers saying, "Will you psychometrise this for me please?"

Holding the slipper in my hand it was clear to me that her mother would soon have to undergo an operation, but how to tell them this? One of my guides said, "You must tell her that a hip operation is necessary."

On telling the wife this, she said, seemingly without surprise, "How soon will it have to be done?"

I replied: "Very soon. In fact, within the next few days." At this, her husband's mouth fell open in astonishment, saying, "Good heavens, you are absolutely right, Sally Jane." Rather sheepishly, he added, "We were just trying to test you, because a letter from the hospital came this morning for my mother-in-law to be admitted." I couldn't have been much closer than that!

When my parents and I went to visit our dear friends, Joy and Norman Cooke, several people, on hearing that we were coming, asked if it would be possible for them to see me at their house, and, of course, I readily agreed.

One of these was a wonderful gentleman called John Norton, MBE, FGS, FRES, who for 30 years had lived for his work as curator of Ludlow Museum, specialising in the natural sciences – geology, zoology and archaeology.

Some months previously, the day before he was to attend a very important meeting of over 120 geologists from all over the world to which he had been greatly looking forward, sadly John suffered a severe heart attack and needed to be resuscitated twice. Although the hospital allowed him to go home after one month of treatment, they warned him he would need plenty of rest, very little exercise and no stress, besides taking about 20 pills a day.

As John entered the room I could see by his aura that he was a very sensitive man, though rather apprehensive and depressed about his present state of health and inactivity.

Smiling, I asked him to sit in front of me, taking both his hands in mine. Almost immediately an elderly, sweet-faced lady with white hair appeared and stood closely beside him. She told me that her name was Great Aunty Mary, and would I please tell John he had been brought back from death for a special reason? There was still important work for him to do in the future. This was to write a book all about his experiences as a museum curator, using all the valuable information he had acquired over the 30 years.

John was absolutely amazed when he heard all this and said: "You have accurately described Great Aunty Mary. She was so close to me and had such a good, loving influence on me during my formative years."

So thrilled was he that he went home and returned shortly afterwards with a large photograph of his aunt, whom I recognised instantly. As John was telling us all about his great aunt, his aura began to brighten and I saw a wonderful change coming over him. I promised to give him absent healing.

Another young lady with many problems also came for a consultation. I was able to help her with some of them, but so numerous were they, and some kept so deeply within her, that getting through the layers was rather like peeling an onion. It would have taken hours to resolve them all so after we got back home the young lady telephoned me several times for further help and Joy tells me that she "can't wait to see Sally Jane again."

How often this happens, wherever I go: someone, somewhere, comes to me for help. It shows quite clearly how much a medium's gifts are needed in this world and how pleased I am to have been given them.

A few days ago, Joy Cooke telephoned me to say that John had come to their home for 'elevenses' and described how he felt when he first met me.

"I felt rather apprehensive, never before having met a medium," John said, "but Sally Jane has such a remarkable ability to soothe with her wonderful calming influence, that soon I felt completely at ease. All the terrible feeling of stress and despondency left me, and have not returned." John continued enthusiastically: "It was really remarkable how Sally Jane was able to bring Great Aunt Mary to me. I have never experienced anything like it in my life. There is no doubt at all that it *was* my great aunt. I shall think very seriously about what she advised me to do regarding writing a book."

The doctor's latest report on John is that he is making an extraordinarily quick recovery.

Here is a letter from Mr. H. W. Williams. It reads:

Dear Sally Jane,

The reading you gave me concerning my wife, Mildred, has given me a great deal of comfort. I was seeking assurance that she had passed over safely, but what a great wealth of data you sent me.

You are so very accurate in your remarks about Mildred and myself, too, that I just had to write and tell you. She did become ill suddenly, with pain in her head and neck. Mildred was writhing about with the pain in her head for three days. She died on the fourth day with a subarachroid massive cerebral haemorrhage. She was only 46 years old, nearly 14 years younger than me.

Mildred was the most wonderful thing that ever happened to me, and all who knew us knew that for a fact. We loved each other dearly and told each other so. We went everywhere together in the seven years and were married on June 4, 1983. I wonder if the seven roses you mention were for those seven years of great happiness.

Yes, Mildred was very methodical and tidy. For 21 years, until we were married, she was a book-keeper for a motor distributor, responsible for all cash, cheques, wages, etc.

You mention that someone who had passed over very suddenly had helped Mildred on to other loved ones; this may have been my nephew Neill. He died of injuries following a motor accident a couple of years ago. He was only 29 years old.

As for myself, yes, I am very strong mentally. I am a survivor. Though there are days when all seems dark and empty I have the strength to throw it aside and get on with the business of living, still with a lot of love in me.

Since receiving your tape I have been able to accept that Mildred is dead. She will not return. Death is irreversible. Had she lived she would have been a cabbage, as you said, and would have hated that.

She dearly loved her mum who died two years ago, also her dad, six years ago. Her little Scottie dog, Jamie, died last year. I am sure now that she is reunited with them all.

Thank you.

Love and Peace,
Hal – H. W. Williams.

## Chapter Twenty-Three

## IN CONCLUSION

THERE are so many things people ask me that shortly I will be making a question-and-answer tape available. Lately, the same question keeps popping up time after time, "Why is it that top mediums like Doris Stokes do not return quickly to tell us all about life in the spirit world?"

Well, my explanation of this is that after all the years of working with Spirit to help mankind they have done their earthly service. In the case of Doris Stokes, she suffered greatly because of ill-health and now needs a resting period of peace and quiet as she passes though the healing process.

I really feel that too much is expected too soon. Remember that when a medium passes, it is exactly the same for them as for anyone else. Mediums are not saints. They do not sprout wings automatically or don haloes. They are simply people who have developed their psychic capabilities to such a high degree of sensitivity that countless numbers of men, women and children here on earth can be healed, advised and comforted.

We must not take it for granted that mediums will want to come back! In the spirit world, as in this one, each spirit has free will to make choices. Mediums, above all people, are completely aware of the beauty and wonders of the next dimension, so who could blame them for wanting to stay there as long as possible?

Picture, if you will, a world of perfection, with no violence, no injustice, no stressful conditions; one, in fact, devoid of all the bad things which we have to tolerate on earth. Imagine a world, somewhat like earth, yet far more beautiful, with absolute peace and tranquillity, for then you will begin to realise why it is that some spirit beings, having been freed of their cumbersome sick body shell, have no wish to return to earthly suffering.

In the early days of my spiritual development, I would ask Grampy Danter and Saint Saba, "What is it like where you live?" One night, they came to my bedside, took both my hands and said, "Come, we will show you."

I remember that astral journey so clearly. It began with being aware of my child spirit rising slowly, weightless and without pain, as they took me to see such wonderful things and beautiful places. "Please," I begged, "why can't I stay here with you and not go back where it hurts me so much to walk?" Saint Saba smiled gently at me and said: "My child, there is so much for you to learn and so much work to be done. One day you will tell the world of this." Of course, at that age, it was all a little beyond my understanding.

As I grew older, Saint Saba told me all about his life on earth. He explained that as far as he was concerned, he had passed away before his task had been completed. However, he did not want to return to another earth life. It was many hundreds of years before he decided to impart all his spiritual knowledge, by becoming a teaching guide to a medium – myself!

Can you imagine his struggle in life? A man who had started Christianity? What inspired him? It was one of a group of guides who are referred to as "The Masters" – those lovely spirits who have returned to earth, life after life, acquiring great wisdom, knowledge and spirituality which they choose to pass on for the benefit of those still here.

Several of my guides were mediums during their lives. One of these is a lady I now know as Mrs White, who was a medium long, long ago in those restricted and unenlightened days, when people with psychic gifts were thought to be witches and burned at the stake. She was a lady with white hair and rosy cheeks, rather short and jolly. She came to me when I was about 11 years old and taught me with Saint Saba what mediumship was all about. When I asked "Whitey" why she chose me to be her vessel she replied, "Because, if you do your work as you should, you will become a medium just like me – direct." This is the way in which I have always worked.

Mrs White told me that when she entered the spirit world after a heart attack, she was met by her husband, the little son she lost as a baby, her parents, grandmother and many others who had loved her. She was very happy for a long time, but later, becoming restless, she went through a period of decision-making whether to return to another earth life. Next time, she was a school teacher in an all-girls school, a lady of very small stature, not at all like her former self, apart from still possessing her psychic capabilities.

Even though this was a century later, mediums were still grossly misunderstood and ridiculed. Most certainly there would have been no freedom for her to have openly written a book about her work. However, Mrs White worked hard at the school, coaching the young girls until she passed away suddenly with a heart attack, just as in her previous life. In the spirit world she was met by the young man she loved and lost.

Each one of my guardian angels has explained to me in detail what had happened to them after their passing. Nanna Watts told me that long before Mama married my stepfather, in spirit she had met Grandfather Edward Danter and they both chose to serve through me.

It pleased Mama and I so very much, when, on returning home after his severe illness, Dadda told us he had become very aware of the presence of his mother, Nanna Watts, and one day had actually seen her beside his bed. Although Mama and I, as mediums, discuss these things quite naturally, now that Dadda has also seen a spirit form for himself it has somehow brought us even closer together as a family.

Living with spirit people is a normal part of my life. It always makes me feel sad to know there are so many persons, going busily about their daily lives, completely unaware of spirit existence. Their days are full of stress, rushing hither and thither, trying to acquire more possessions and status. They will not go out of their way to help anybody but themselves. If only they knew the truth, the deeper meaning and purpose of life!

Occasionally, in the course of my work, a spirit visitor will come to me saying rather sheepishly, "I was a complete agnostic, who wouldn't listen to anyone who tried to tell me that there was a next world, but have since found out how very wrong I was."

One of the several reasons for writing this book is in the hope that it will help people to understand that no matter who, or what we are, all of us will return to the spirit world, which is not "somewhere up there" but all around us.

Looking back over my life, I can honestly say that my guides have never been known to tell me, or those who come for help, anything other than the truth.

As always, Saint Saba was right. Someone *did* come into my life to write a book about me and my work. She is my dear friend, Joy Cooke. And until two years ago neither of us knew of the other's existence.

When Joy wrote to me for a taped reading, as I held the photograph of herself, her husband Norman and daughter Linda, I knew with certainty that this family and mine would become as one, for there has been so much in their lives similar to ours.

Linda was born with cerebral palsy and is badly incapacitated, needing constant supervision, care and attention, which is lovingly given by her parents. They know only too well, as do my parents, exactly what it means to have someone they love completely reliant on them – the great responsibility of it, the restrictions on their personal lives and all the fears for the future.

As I was recording Joy's tape I could feel the deep depression and desperation which had prompted her to write to me. Diane, standing beside me, said, "Tell her that she must take up writing again."

Now, there was no way I could possibly have known of Joy's past success as a short story writer, but because of extra demands made on her owing to family illness she found it impossible to continue.

It was clear that Joy had a deep understanding of all things spiritual and psychic, the only one in her family who had inherited "awareness" from a mediumistic grandmother.

My guides brought Joy's well-loved sister in spirit to her. She had been silent, making no communication whatever since her passing four years ago. Later, Joy telephoned to thank me for giving her a new outlook on life. During our conversation she said: "The whole subject intrigues me so much that whenever I hear of a new autobiography written by a medium soon to be published I immediately order a copy. Have you written your autobiography yet, Sally Jane?"

At this point, Saint Saba and Grampy Danter appeared, smiling their approval as I replied: "No, but numerous people have offered to do so though I have not, so far, found the right person, until now. Would you like to do it, Joy?"

There was a gasp at the other end of the telephone. "Oh, Sally Jane, I don't know whether I could, for somehow there has only been time for short stories," said Joy regretfully.

"Well," I assured her, "you are perfectly capable and will write it." That was how it all came about.

Working together, we have written "Guardian Angels" with love, understanding and compassion for the troubles which beset our fellow human beings, to try to show people how life does continue after death. Can people really imagine that those who have loved them in their earthly life could possibly leave them when they have passed into the spirit world? No, they do not! Even though their physical presence is no longer visible, nothing will keep them away in times of trouble, sickness and unhappiness. Mediumship is one of God's greatest gifts to mankind, for it is through our eyes, ears and speech that we are able to prove immortality.

Saint Saba has told me that there is a long earthly road ahead of me. He was also right about the number of people who want me to teach them how to develop their psychic capabilities like psychometry, meditation and relaxation classes, auragraph interpretations and past life recall.

All this will be a wonderful step forward in my work, which I eagerly anticipate, knowing that my guides will be forever with me.

I have entitled this book "Guardian Angels Around My Bed" – for this is exactly what they are.

## TRIBUTE TO DADDA

Whilst this book was in the final stages of its production, my darling Dadda passed on. Of course, Mama and I were deeply saddened and miss his physical presence. But how blessed we are to know that Dadda is still very much around, and is just a thought away. I know he will do all he can from the spirit realms to guide and protect us.

You see, those joined by a link of love can never truly be separated for love conquers all, even death.

I realise that Dadda is now with Saint Saba, Grampy Danter and all my other helpers, friends and relatives in the Larger Life, and that when my time comes to leave this earth plane he will be amongst the first to greet me, with arms outstretched. What a joy and a privilege our priceless knowledge of spiritual realities is. And once you have a faith founded on psychic knowledge no one – and nothing – can ever take that away from you.

Dadda, I love you dearly. God be with you.

Your adoring Sally Jane.

## END NOTE
### By Joy Cooke

I WAS so intrigued when Sally Jane told me about Saint Saba that I asked the help of our very friendly Ludlow Librarian, Jenny Smallman, who after making a search, sent me photocopies taken from several books which gave us all a clear picture of his life and work. Sally Jane and her mother were delighted to read all about their well-loved guide.

There is also a book entitled "Saints of the East" by Donald Attwater, which has interested us very much.

Little did I realise on the day my taped reading arrived, and my subsequent phone call to Sally Jane, what wonderful changes would take place in my family as well as in her own, things which up until that time had been only pipe dreams suddenly turned into reality! Life has taken on quite a different meaning for me.

There is no doubt at all that whoever meets this lovely lady agrees that as a medium she is in a class of her own.